The British Constitution: A Very Short Introduction

VERY SHORT INTRODUCTIONS are for anyone wanting a stimulating and accessible way into a new subject. They are written by experts, and have been translated into more than 45 different languages.

The series began in 1995, and now covers a wide variety of topics in every discipline. The VSI library currently contains over 700 volumes—a Very Short Introduction to everything from Psychology and Philosophy of Science to American History and Relativity—and continues to grow in every subject area.

Very Short Introductions available now:

Available soon:

For more information visit our website

www.oup.com/vsi/

Martin Loughlin

THE BRITISH CONSTITUTION

A Very Short Introduction

SECOND EDITION

OXFORD
UNIVERSITY PRESS

OXFORD
UNIVERSITY PRESS

Great Clarendon Street, Oxford, OX2 6DP,
United Kingdom

Oxford University Press is a department of the University of Oxford.
It furthers the University's objective of excellence in research, scholarship,
and education by publishing worldwide. Oxford is a registered trade mark of
Oxford University Press in the UK and in certain other countries

© Martin Loughlin 2023

The moral rights of the author have been asserted

First edition published in 2013

All rights reserved. No part of this publication may be reproduced, stored in
a retrieval system, or transmitted, in any form or by any means, without the
prior permission in writing of Oxford University Press, or as expressly permitted
by law, by licence or under terms agreed with the appropriate reprographics
rights organization. Enquiries concerning reproduction outside the scope of the
above should be sent to the Rights Department, Oxford University Press, at the
address above

You must not circulate this work in any other form
and you must impose this same condition on any acquirer

Published in the United States of America by Oxford University Press
198 Madison Avenue, New York, NY 10016, United States of America

British Library Cataloguing in Publication Data
Data available

Library of Congress Control Number: 2023936251

ISBN 978-0-19-289525-7

Printed and bound by
CPI Group (UK) Ltd, Croydon, CR0 4YY

Links to third party websites are provided by Oxford in good faith and
for information only. Oxford disclaims any responsibility for the materials
contained in any third party website referenced in this work.

Contents

Preface

The purpose of this book is to explain the workings of the British constitution by setting it in a broad historical context. Written over a decade ago, it was anticipated that it might stand the test of time. Subsequent events, however, have raised more profound questions of constitutional significance than during any other decade since the First World War. A new edition considering these developments seems necessary.

The book was initially written during the early phase of the 2010–15 Conservative–Liberal Democrat Coalition government, whose joint *Programme for Government* opened with the dramatic statement: 'The Government believes that our political system is broken.' After promising a series of ambitious constitutional reforms, the achievements of the Coalition government fell considerably short of expectation. There was no reform of the voting system, no equalization of constituencies, no reform of the House of Lords, and no reform or repeal of the Human Rights Act. The Prime Minister's discretionary power to dissolve Parliament had been curbed by the Fixed-terms Parliament Act 2011, though it was not self-evident that this measure—designed to protect the junior partner—would improve the system of government. In 2019, it contributed to a breakdown in parliamentary arrangements and has since been repealed.

The most significant innovation was to recognize the value of holding a referendum before proceeding with major reform, although in the event its most dramatic usage—the independence referendum held in Scotland in 2014—had been initiated by the Scottish government and only reluctantly conceded by the Coalition government. When the Conservatives were returned in 2015 with an overall majority, however, they quickly employed a referendum to gauge popular support for continued membership of the European Union. And it is the shock result of that exercise that initiated an unprecedented period of constitutional unsettlement that continues to reverberate today.

Implementation of the Brexit referendum result caused a major upheaval in Britain's system of parliamentary government. This has been reflected in the breakdown of many conventions of constitutional government and a renewed pressure to convert informal practices into formal rules. But the depth of this unsettlement can also be measured by the fact that, despite continuous Conservative rule since 2015, the UK has had four different Prime Ministers only one of whom took office by winning a general election and, other than the present (2023) incumbent, none of whom has been removed by defeat in a general election.

In these unsettled conditions, it seemed as if the only thing holding together the United Kingdom of Great Britain and Northern Ireland was the continuing dignified presence of Queen Elizabeth II. Her death in September 2022 after seventy years on the throne now signifies the passing of an era that from a constitutional perspective has marked the progressive decline in governmental authority.

But the future is not my subject. The purpose of this new edition is to bring the story of Britain's constitutional development up to date. In completing it, I am indebted to Pravar Petkar for research assistance and to Chris Foley for having helped to make it more readable.

List of illustrations

Chapter 1
The existential question

Is there a British constitution?

Once extolled as a standing wonder, the British constitution today
evokes bewilderment and even derision. Many now find the idea
of a constitution that has grown organically simply puzzling.
A century ago, the historian Sidney Low claimed that 'we live
under a system of tacit understandings', though these 'are not
always understood'. Today the problem is not confined to grasping
the meaning of these tacit constitutional understandings: the
question is whether they still exist.

The British clearly have a system of government, a set of rules
regulating the exercise of political power. But the idea of a
constitution connotes something more. It suggests that
institutions of government are infused with values and modes of
conduct that fix the meaning of those rules and express a distinct
way of organizing political life. Do such values and practices still
exist? Do they still command authority? It is in this deeper sense
that we ask whether there is still such a thing as a British
constitution.

There is every reason to answer that question affirmatively, not
least because this book would otherwise rank as the shortest of all

Very Short Introductions. But the evidence of the last five decades is not reassuring.

Since the 1970s from across the political spectrum there has been growing dissatisfaction with constitutional arrangements. Consider Lord Hailsham's celebrated 1976 Dimbleby Lecture on *Elective Dictatorship*. Opening with the paradox that government had never before possessed so much power and commanded so little respect, he noted that there was scarcely an institution of government that did not come in for serious criticism. For Hailsham, this was because these institutions were no longer performing their constitutional role of providing a balance: the monarchy had been reduced to an entirely ceremonial function, the House of Lords no longer acted as a restraining influence, and political conduct was determined by party political interest rather than any sense of constitutionally appropriate behaviour. Customary constitutional restraints were no longer working and traditions of civility from which these constitutional values have evolved were losing authority. The only solution, Hailsham concluded, was to devise an entirely new constitution, which, like all new constitutions, must be written down and defined by law.

Hailsham was hardly a radical. Son of a viscount, educated at Eton and Oxford, after practising at the bar he had a successful career as a Conservative MP and Minister. And once the Conservatives were returned to office in 1979, Hailsham, now Lord Chancellor, quietly shelved his proposal: restructuring government became more important than reforming the constitution.

Hailsham's theme was quickly taken up by a breakaway Labour group who in 1981 founded a new party. At the heart of the programme of the Social Democratic Party was a proposal for fundamental constitutional reform, elaborated by David Marquand in *The Unprincipled Society* (1988). Marquand argued that Britain's problems—economic as well as political—stem from the failure of its political class to shed a Victorian constitutional mentality. Whereas Hailsham had proposed a modern constitution to protect the Victorian values that Conservatives hold dear, Marquand was criticizing their pervasive influence. The problem, he contended, is that we are living in a society in which property is an antecedent right, liberty is realized when we are left alone, and government is best left in the hands of an experienced political elite conscious of its obligations to society. The past genius of the traditional constitution has become the source of our present weaknesses. The British problem, he concluded, was one of maladaptation; fundamental constitutional reform was needed so that modern ideas of democracy and citizenship rights could flourish.

Marquand's message was later adopted by the 1990s Labour party which, reformed and rebranded as 'new Labour', won the 1997 election on a platform of constitutional modernization. It quickly introduced new measures of constitutional significance: governmental power was devolved to Scotland, Wales, and Northern Ireland, the House of Lords was reformed, and innovations such as the Human Rights Act and the Freedom of Information Act were adopted. This was the most radical set of constitutional reforms promoted by any government since the First World War.

These reforms nevertheless provoked unsettling questions. Wasn't this package rather makeshift? Was the new constitutional settlement coherent? Didn't these reforms leave untouched the exercise of power at the centre? Did the programme not in fact demonstrate the impossibility of governments themselves reordering constitutional fundamentals? Political analyst Will Hutton had already indicated the difficulties. In *The State We're In* (1995), he explained how economic and political changes since the 1970s had eroded the public service ethos that bolstered traditional arrangements. But he also recognized that the sort of fundamental constitutional reform now required had never before been achieved by any nation without the utter collapse of its system of government.

The European venture

By the twenty-first century, there seemed to be a broad-based consensus that Britain's inherited constitution had come to the end of its useful life. Constitutional reform had secured a prominent but highly ambivalent place on the agendas of all major political parties. But there was one dimension of recent developments that had been overlooked. The most powerful driving force of constitutional modernization over the last several decades has been the United Kingdom's participation in the venture of continuing European integration. This involvement has empowered the judiciary to extend rights-based methods of review, meaning that the British have adopted what is in effect a Bill of Rights without the need for extensive public deliberation. It has also helped set in place a dynamic scheme for devolving governmental powers to the constituent nations of the UK as well as bolstering the unique cross-border arrangements that brought about a peace settlement in Northern Ireland. Continuing European integration has enabled governing arrangements to be re-configured and constitutional fundamentals re-ordered so as to bring the UK into closer alignment with the frameworks of modern constitutional democracies.

This European aspect reveals the depth of the contemporary crisis of constitutional practice. The UK's 2016 referendum decision to withdraw from the European Union has led to a protracted period of unsettlement, the constitutional implications of which did not end on 31 January 2020 when the UK formally left the EU. These broad-reaching repercussions flow from the fact that European integration has been fostered not only by membership of the EU but also by adherence, through membership of the Council of Europe, to the European Convention on Human Rights.

The impact of these current developments means that interest in constitutional questions has never been greater and their uncertainty never deeper. Recent reforms initiated by both domestic and European developments have led to the codification of many of the rules. In this sense, the British are closer than ever to having a written constitution. At the same time, however, the common values this rule-system is supposed to uphold have become increasingly unclear. It is in this sense that the existential question—does Britain possess a constitution?—remains real.

One important initial task must be to consider how the present predicament was reached. This book therefore begins by outlining the basic features of the traditional constitution and explaining how it survived into the modern world. Why, when all other nations were adopting formal documentary statements of their constitutional arrangements, did the British maintain these traditional arrangements? In later chapters, I examine the tensions that emerge in trying to operate in a world of modern government with a heritage of traditional constitutional forms and consider how scholars have addressed the challenge of writing about the unwritten constitution. I will also explain how the constitution changes once the English state is transformed into the British state, then acquires and subsequently loses an empire. And I will examine the implications of the UK's integration into, and subsequent exit from, the European Union.

Chapter 2
What constitution?

The British are almost unique in not having a written constitution.
What does this mean? It cannot mean that governing
arrangements are not laid down in writing. If the constitution is
defined as the rules that establish and regulate the institutions of
government, then the British do have a set of such rules. The
unusual feature of the British constitution is only that these rules
have not been gathered together in a document called 'the
Constitution'. Is this the deficiency contemporary reformers seek
to remedy? Is constitutional modernization driven by the desire to
systematize these rules and present them in a single document?

That would be an over-simplification. The difficulties touch on
more fundamental questions. During the 18th century, the British
were feted for having the 'matchless constitution', one that
managed to combine the virtues of monarchy, aristocracy, and
democracy while avoiding their characteristic vices. And
throughout the 19th century, the constitution was admired for its
ability to facilitate the transition to modern parliamentary
democracy by incremental adjustment without the need for
violent revolution. The constitution was felt to express not only a
set of rules but, more fundamentally, the values of the political
nation. So it appears that contemporary difficulties come not just
from an apparent desire to codify the rules but, more profoundly,

from a need to restate and rekindle the values on which the modern polity rests.

One of the basic confusions arising from this debate stems from ambiguity over the meaning of the term 'constitution'. In the history of political constitutions, some discrepancy has arisen between traditional and modern understandings. Since the British have a historic, customary, evolutionary—i.e. traditional—constitution, we should begin by considering this distinction.

The traditional idea of the constitution

Writing in 1830, the great German philosopher G. W. F. Hegel asserted that 'what is called "making" a "constitution" is a thing that has never happened in history'. The constitution of a state, he argued, is not merely a set of institutional arrangements but a cultural artefact that 'develops from the national spirit'. In this traditional understanding, the constitution expresses a nation's culture, customs, and values as much as its system of government. The constitution is not some dish that can be made from a recipe. It can no more be made than language is made; like language, the constitution evolves through usage. It expresses the ways in which we conceive ourselves as a 'people' or a 'nation' or, when focusing on our governing arrangements, as a 'state'.

One of the most influential exponents of this traditional sense of the constitution was Edmund Burke. Burke's views are most prominently expressed in *Reflections on the Revolution in France* (1790), the purpose of which was to warn of the dangers of engaging in radical constitutional reconstruction in the wake of the 1789 Revolution. A political constitution, Burke argued, is 'an entailed inheritance' derived from 'our forefathers' and transmitted to posterity. It is 'a liberal descent': the British respect institutions established over time and seek to improve them incrementally, but if not entirely obsolete they also seek to retain them. Only through such prudent and incremental reform can the constitution work within the grain of social and political development and become a living reality.

Burke's point is that when constitution-making is reduced to a rationalist exercise in construction all the 'pleasing illusions which made power gentle and obedience liberal' are dissolved. If 'ancient opinions and rules of life are taken away', the loss is inestimable. Lacking a compass to govern us, we cannot know in which direction to steer, and we fall into a condition of ceaseless change. Constitutional government works, he is saying, not because of the symmetry of some formal rule-based design but by the gradual emergence of customary ways of conduct that channel the exercise of power through certain ceremonies and forms. Strip away the mystique and you remove the behavioural constraints that make the exercise of governing power benign. Remove the sacred from the constitutional and 'the whole chain and continuity of the commonwealth' is broken. Treat the state as a mechanism that can be made and re-made in accordance with the 'floating fancies or fashions' and the very basis of political authority is lost.

For Burke, the task of maintaining the constitution requires a grasp of human nature and human necessities, together with knowledge of what facilitates or obstructs the various ends pursued by governing institutions. This practical art draws on the experience of a governing elite acquired through traditions handed down over many generations. It is not a task to be derived from some philosophical template. The constitution is 'a partnership not only between those who are living, but between those who are living, those who are dead, and those who are to be born'. Indeed, in this traditional understanding, the better the constitution the fewer the written constitutional laws, since laws only reinforce a mode of conduct that has not been fully absorbed in the manners, traditions, and practices of a people.

The modern idea of the constitution

Some might say that Hegel was wrong about 'making' constitutions. During the summer of 1787, delegates from the thirteen American states had met in Philadelphia to draft a new Federal Constitution for the United States. 'After the lapse of 6,000 years since the creation of the world', wrote James Wilson, 'America now presents the first instance of a people assembled to weigh deliberately and calmly, to decide leisurely and peaceably, upon the form of government by which they will bind themselves and their posterity.' The US Constitution was the world's first modern written constitution. Its adoption opened a new era in constitutional development. Thereafter, at certain critical points in their history, nations began adopting written constitutions.

The founders of the modern American republic were conscious of making a new type of constitution. In the first of *The Federalist Papers*, the journalistic effort by leading framers to persuade the voters of New York to ratify the new Constitution, Alexander Hamilton observed that it was 'reserved to the people of this country' to decide whether societies are 'capable or not of establishing good government from reflection and choice' or whether they were 'destined to depend for their political constitutions on accident and force'. In place of the idea that the traditional constitution expressed a nation's traditions and ethical practices, Hamilton was arguing that it rested on vagaries of 'accident and force', on power interests rather than cultural commitments. Contrary to Burke's claim that the constitution was an 'inheritance', a set of practices consecrated by custom and received by a people, Hamilton maintained it was an instrument by which 'the people', after reasoned debate, agree the terms on which they are governed.

Thomas Paine immediately recognized the revolutionary nature of this shift. 'It is not sufficient that we adopt the word', he declaimed, 'we must fix also a standard specification to it.' In his *Rights of Man* of 1791, Paine provided the first clear statement of the modern idea of a constitution, stressing four key features:

1. The constitution must have a real rather than virtual existence; it is a thing and, specifically, a *document*.
2. The constitution is a thing *antecedent to a government*. Since it establishes the government, the constitution cannot be made by government, but only by 'the people'.
3. The constitution must specify all the powers and duties of the government: it must be *comprehensive*.
4. The constitution has the status of *fundamental law*. Being the law of law-making, the constitution is a higher form of law. Since this body of constitutional law is not made by the governing institutions but by the people to establish those institutions, governments and legislatures have no authority to alter constitutional law.

This modern concept of a constitution has since been adopted across the world. Nearly 200 nation-states, along with many sub-national units (provinces, states, etc.) in federal regimes, now have written constitutions of the modern type—documents that define and limit the powers of the institutions of government and which take effect as fundamental law.

Traditional v. modern

Modern constitutions possess varying degrees of authority. It would be wrong to take the US Constitution as the epitome of the modern concept. Drafted in 1787, since 1791, when the first ten Amendments were attached as the Bill of Rights, it has been amended only seventeen times and is now regarded as set in stone. By contrast, the French have adopted at least twelve different constitutions since their Revolution of 1789 and have experienced dictatorship, monarchy, and five republics.

The French experience is more typical. Only a handful of national constitutions pre-date the Second World War and most of the current constitutions have been newly adopted, or fundamentally amended, since 1989.

This variable experience should caution against any assumption that the modern constitution has altogether replaced the traditional idea. Standards for governmental decision-making laid down in written constitutions express ideal aspirations but often tell us little about the way power is exercised. Indeed, the constitution might simply be a façade that masks stark realities. But even if the norms laid down in the text are fully complied with, they only regulate the office of government. Behind the shadow lies the substance: behind *government* lies the *state* itself—the way we conceive the political unity of a people.

The essential point is that the traditional and modern concepts have different objects. The modern constitution has as its object the office of government, while the traditional concept has that of the state. The modern concept distinguishes between government and society, whereas the traditional concept suggests that the manners, culture, and traditions of a people form the 'real' constitution of the state.

Experience indicates that the task of drafting a constitution of the modern type is not so difficult. Though coming in different styles, they tend to follow a common template. The US Constitution remains a model of concision. The first article establishes a national bicameral legislature (the Congress); the second, a national executive (the President); the third, a national judicature (the Supreme Court); the fourth, the relationship with the states; the fifth, the amending procedure; the sixth, the treatment of public debt; and the seventh (and last), the procedure for ratification. But drafting and adopting such a constitution does not make it a living reality. That task lies ahead.

The great challenge for a state adopting a new constitution is to ensure that its principles and values are embraced by its people. The challenge is to foster a political culture that upholds the standing of the constitution. The case of 20th-century Germany is instructive. The social democratic Weimar Constitution of 1919 failed because, in the fraught circumstances of defeat in the First World War and the removal of the monarchy, many political parties did not accept the authority of the new constitution. One of the great achievements of the German people since the Second World War, by contrast, has been to live up to the values and procedures of a federal constitution that was effectively imposed on them by the Allies.

Modern constitutions serve both instrumental and symbolic purposes. As instruments of government, they establish the procedures of public decision-making. As symbolic documents, they provide a symbol of unity and identity. In their instrumental role, they are geared to the future, but in their symbolic function they draw on the past, on heroic stories about the vicissitudes of a virtuous people. These 'mere scraps of paper' are transformed into authoritative—almost sacred—texts only if both aspects are aligned. This suggests that the constitution can fully realize its ambition only when it functions in harmony with the customs of the people. The constitution of the office of government (the modern idea) must be consonant with that of the constitution of the state (the traditional idea).

The traditional constitution is invariably less precise with respect to instrumental guidance; after all, it generally draws on custom and practice rather than formally promulgated rules. But these evolving practices reflect changes in the political culture of the nation, which can radically alter the character of formal constitutional settlements. In this sense, the 'real' constitution of the United States—the ways in which power is today legitimately exercised in practice—might be just as unwritten as that of the United Kingdom.

Why doesn't Britain have a modern constitution?

Since the modern concept is now so prevalent, it is widely assumed that, adhering to the traditional type, the British do not even have a constitution. This view was even being openly expressed in the 19th century. 'In England the constitution may change continually', noted Tocqueville in 1835, and it therefore 'does not in reality exist'. Why is this?

The modern constitution is the product of the Enlightenment, a movement that flourished throughout Europe during the mid- to late 18th century. Sometimes called 'the Age of Reason', the Enlightenment expressed a secular, scientific, rationalist spirit and left its mark on the arts, the sciences, religion, and politics. It also left its imprint—especially in its aspiration of freedom from arbitrary power—on both the American and French revolutions.

Since the late 18th century, modern constitutions have been adopted by many nations at critical moments in their history, largely because of some major crisis that has shaken the foundations of governmental authority. They are commonly drafted in the aftermath of defeat in war or on the success of a revolutionary movement in overthrowing the old order, or because a new state has been formed through the break-up of old empires. They symbolize the opening of a new chapter in the nation's history or the birth of a new nation-state.

As it happens, since the 18th century the British have made the transition to modernity without revolutionary insurrection. Indeed, some would say that this is precisely because of the flexibility of their traditional constitution. They have also been fortunate not to have suffered the ignomy of defeat in war. Consequently, while British lawyers have acquired considerable experience in drafting constitutions for former colonies that have negotiated independence since the Second World War, they have never had occasion to examine their own constitutional fundamentals and codify the British constitution in a single authoritative document.

An alternative way of looking at this history might be to note that the British—strictly, the English—had their political revolution too early. In English political history, the era of revolutionary upheaval was the 17th rather than the 18th century. During the 1640s, civil war raged in England and after the defeat of the Royalist cause in 1649 the king—Charles I—was executed and a Commonwealth formed. During this latter period, a written constitution was drafted. The Instrument of Government of 1653, which created new governing arrangements by placing legislative power in Parliament and executive power in a Lord Protector (Oliver Cromwell) and his Council, could be viewed as the first written constitution of a modern nation-state. But this constitution did not establish a comprehensive framework of government and for this reason it cannot be treated as a constitution of the modern type. The governing arrangements that were instituted also suggested that the revolutionaries responsible for executing the king still believed in the office of the king. Unsuccessful attempts were made to persuade Cromwell to assume the crown and following his death in 1658 the regime soon unravelled. In 1660, the dominant faction restored the monarchy by inviting Charles II to take his father's throne.

A further upheaval occurred in 1688. In 1685, Charles II was succeeded by his younger brother, James. James II wanted to institute a programme of absolutist Catholic modernization modelled on the French regime of Louis XIV. Faced with this threat to the traditional constitution, the Whig aristocracy enlisted the help of William of Orange, who was married to James's Protestant daughter Mary. When William landed in England at the head of a Dutch army, James fled the country. The ruling elite determined that James had forfeited the crown. They then held a convention Parliament without the king who should have summoned it and invited William and Mary to reign jointly.

Once again, the terms of this new constitutional settlement were drafted in a formal document. But the Bill of Rights of 1689 was merely the statement of a resolution of grievances that Parliament held against the government. The events of 1688 signal the world's first modern revolution. Yet the Bill of Rights, while not itself amounting to a modern constitution, did pave the way for a modern constitutional arrangement based on what might be called a parliamentary state. The significance of 1688 is complicated by the fact that the language of the revolutionary settlement was thoroughly conservative: the settlement was presented as the restoration of the traditional constitution whose workings had been undermined by the actions of the Stuart kings. In reality, it amounted to an aristocratic coup d'état and it resulted in the balance of power shifting from crown to Parliament. In masking this fact, the language of the 1688 settlement set the tone of subsequent discourse: thereafter, modernizing changes were invariably dressed up in a rhetoric of constitutional conservation.

Since the 17th century, there has been no fundamental breakdown in governmental authority that would cause the English to reconstitute themselves politically. But this does not mean there have been no basic changes in the structure of the state. Since the 17th century, we have seen the transformation of England into the state of Great Britain in 1707, and then in 1800 the formation of the United Kingdom of Great Britain and Ireland, and after 1920 the United Kingdom of Great Britain and Northern Ireland.

The United Kingdom now forms a complex, pluri-national state. The English state was centralized following the Norman Conquest of 1066, and thereafter the key strategic objective was to maintain the security of England's borders by subjugating the other nations of the British Isles. With respect to Wales, this process was complete by 1535 when Wales was absorbed into the English shire structure: the English state incorporated Wales, and the English common law was applied throughout England and Wales. The position with respect to Scotland and Ireland is less simple. Scotland was not conquered; instead, in 1707 England entered into the Treaty of Union with Scotland to form the state of Great Britain. Relations with Ireland are even more complicated, but all that need be said presently is that the Union with Ireland Act 1800 abolished the Irish Parliament and provided for Irish representation in the new Parliament of the United Kingdom of Great Britain and Ireland. On each occasion, these treaties formally established a new state. Why, then, did they not lead to a modern constitutional settlement?

Consider the Scottish case. The Treaty of Union provided for Scottish representation in the English Parliament and contained protections for aspects of Scots public identity, especially law, Church, and education. There has recently evolved in Scotland a romantic view that this is a constitutional treaty in the modern sense. Yet the evidence suggests that it was an incorporating exercise: the effect of the Treaty was to incorporate Scotland into the governing framework of the English state. Those who suggest otherwise make a historically anachronistic argument: to read the Treaty of 1707 through post-Enlightenment constitutional spectacles might be good rhetoric but it is bad law. In engineering this union, the English deliberately avoided—for reasons of state—opening up for consideration any fundamental constitutional questions.

The policy of the English governing class with respect to the Anglo-Scottish Union is one reason why governmental developments since the 17th century have never resulted in constitutional renewal. The English governing temperament has always militated against any serious enquiry into the first principles of constitutional practice. The vagaries of historical development provide one explanation for this, but it is not the only one. We might also consider the temperament of the English.

The spirit of the British constitution

It is often said that the characteristic virtue of the English is their fixation on the practical, while their distinctive vice is an unwillingness to gauge their achievements in terms of principle. The English—and indeed British—maintain an empiricist and pragmatic disposition. Suspicion of abstract speculation threads its way through the traditions of British philosophy from Bacon, Hobbes, and Locke to Hume, Bentham, and Mill. It is rooted in uncompromising matter-of-factness, a tendency to weigh up knowledge against utility. This pragmatic and anti-Rationalist temperament has left its imprint on matters of politics, government, and constitution.

Burke is a great exemplar of this disposition. In his essay on the French Revolution, he argued that, as with all true constitutions, the British constitution had been sustained by a distrust of abstract principles. Political institutions are too complex to be governed according to principles that take no account of time, place, or circumstance. Politics must be adapted 'not to human reason, but to human nature, of which reason is but a part and not the greatest part'. In his essay *On the Present Discontents* (1770), he explained that nations are not primarily ruled by laws, and even less by force. Rather, they are governed by a judicious management of 'the temper of the people'. However government is formally constituted, 'infinitely the greater part of it must depend upon the exercise of the powers that are left at large to the prudence and uprightness of ministers of state'. Without this temper, the 'commonwealth is no better than a scheme upon paper; and not a living, active, effective constitution'.

The 20th-century philosopher who did most to explain constitutional implications was Michael Oakeshott. In

Rationalism in Politics (1962), Oakeshott highlighted the superiority of the English approach, pointing to the deficiencies of the Rationalist mentality underpinning the idea of the modern constitution. The Rationalist, he argues, is 'the enemy of authority, of prejudice, of the merely traditional, customary or habitual'. Nothing is of value merely because it exists; there is no opinion, custom, or belief that is not to be measured by the power of the Rationalist's reason. The cumulation of experience is registered only when rendered orderly, distinct, and converted to a formula. Politics becomes a type of engineering. The notion of founding a state upon a Declaration of the Rights of Man is a typical product of the Rationalist brain. But the error of Rationalism is that of discounting practical knowledge, knowledge acquired from experience, and believing only in scientific knowledge—the precise formulation in rules and principles which can be written down, taught, and learned.

Oakeshott's primary concern is how the Rationalist disposition had come to shape modern political practice. He deplored the extent to which 'traditions of behaviour have given place to ideologies, the extent to which the politics of destruction and creation have been substituted for the politics of repair, the consciously planned and deliberately executed being considered (for that reason) better than what has grown up and established itself unselfconsciously over a period of time'. His argument that politics, as a tradition of behaviour, was being replaced by doctrine and technique also has specific constitutional implications.

The American colonists—a society of 'self-made men'—took the analysis that Locke and others had distilled from the English political tradition and converted it into a set of doctrines based on abstract principles. The Declaration of Independence takes its place alongside the French Declaration of Rights as one of the sacred documents of Rationalist politics, and one of the founding texts of the modern concept of constitution. In contrast, the English tradition exemplified in Magna Carta (1215), the Petition of Right (1628), or the Bill of Rights (1689) had been to declare and corroborate the old rather than make the new. But those late 18th-century documents sanctified universal principles rather than traditional practices. Rights that had been the fruits of custom and practice were transplanted into the new world, where they were declared to be the product of 'nature'. What was exported as 'the concrete rights of an Englishman', Oakeshott argues, 'have returned home as the abstract Rights of Man, and they have returned to confound our politics and corrupt our minds'. He contends that modern constitutions are not merely codifications attributable to modern circumstances; they are products of a Rationalism that has distorted the legacy of the evolutionary British constitution.

The spirit of the constitution finds expression in the practices of English common law, a body of ancient custom—a set of usages, practices, and rulings that have evolved from time immemorial. The common law is 'unwritten law', with the authority of the judicial decision being limited to what has actually been decided rather than standing for some general principle that might seem logically to follow from it. As Chief Justice Coke was obliged to inform James I at the beginning of the 17th century, the common law is a type of 'artificial reason' which 'requires long study and experience before that a man can attain to the cognizance of it'. Its spirit is incorporated in the practices of the bar, where competence is acquired not by scholastic education but by apprenticeship to a pupil master, during which the pupil learns the techniques of drafting and pleading, acquiring the sort of practical knowledge that can be distilled only from experienced advocacy. And this tradition is bolstered by the profession of a cloistered judiciary, drawn from the ranks of senior barristers and working not from general principle but from precedent to precedent (see Box).

The British constitution is, arguably, the product of the extension of common-law method to the activity of governing: unwritten

The method of common law

Lord Halsbury, *Quinn v Leatham* [1901] AC 495, 506: 'A case is only an authority for what it actually decides. I entirely deny that it can be quoted for a proposition that may seem to follow logically from it. Such a mode of reasoning assumes that the law is necessarily a logical code, whereas every lawyer must acknowledge that the law is not always logical at all.'

law simply mutates into the idea of the unwritten constitution. If we try to convert the traditional constitution into something analogous to the modern concept—to treat it as a set of rules establishing and regulating the activity of governing—the constitution appears quite random. It seems to be a miscellaneous collection of statutes, rules, and guidelines, none of which constitutes 'higher law' and many of which make little sense until interpreted in the light of innumerable political understandings. This argument also highlights the ambiguities about whether the British constitution is actually an English constitution. At heart, that constitution is simply an assemblage of customary practices, with the 'rules' often amounting to no more than cribs distilled from such practices. This is a traditional constitution, an inheritance, a partnership between past, present, and future.

This traditional idea of the constitution generates a number of questions to be taken up in the chapters that follow:

- Given Britain's peculiar heritage, how have scholars addressed the challenge of writing about the unwritten constitution? Presenting a clear account of its workings is some task, not least because a constitution that thrives on ambiguity and informality must constantly intertwine political and constitutional questions. This is addressed in Chapter 3.

- What gives the British constitution its distinctive character? This is answered in Chapter 4, which focuses on the practices that shape the British tradition of parliamentary government.
- How does the constitution change once the English state is transformed into the British state, then acquires and subsequently loses an empire? And what are the implications of reconfiguring the governing arrangements of the several nations of the United Kingdom and of integration into, and subsequent exit from, the European Union? The consequences of these territorial changes are addressed in Chapter 5.
- The great virtue of the 'matchless constitution' was its apparent ability to reconcile order and liberty: the British constitution aspired to be the 'constitution of liberty'. How is civil liberty protected? How is it maintained in the face of pressures arising from the extension of administrative government? These issues are addressed in Chapter 6.
- What remains of the traditional constitution? The concluding chapter brings together the preceding concerns: the incipient Rationalism of written rules, the waning of parliamentary authority, the reconfiguring of identities following changing territorial arrangements, and the erosion of civil liberty. It considers whether Rationalism is now the driving force, reflects on the consequences of Brexit, and considers the prospects for adopting a modern entrenched British constitution.

Chapter 3
Writing the constitution

The British treat their constitution as the inheritance of a long tradition in the practical art of governing. Understandably, they have been reluctant to commit its basic rules to writing. If constitutional understanding is acquired through experience, the type of knowledge it embodies is not easily expressed in books or conveyed through formal instruction. Since formal rules are not the source of constitutional behaviour, codification of the constitution would change it. British government does, of course, operate in accordance with rules, but mainly rules of procedure and precedent rather than of principle.

Throughout the 18th and 19th centuries, many extolled the virtues of the British constitution without being at all clear about the way it worked. For those of a scientific temperament, this could be most frustrating. Yet a certain group of scholars—those coming from abroad—became very interested in unlocking the secret of the constitution, not least because they were intrigued to understand how the British had made the transition to modernity without undergoing violent revolution. The works of such distinguished European jurists as Montesquieu, de Lolme, von Gneist, and Redlich provide some of the most penetrating insights into the nature of the British constitution, even when revealing as much about their own political concerns as about the actualities of British governing practices. Many readers come away from their studies confirmed in the view that the constitution rests on some ineffable British genius in matters political.

To the extent that the British wrote about their own constitution, these were mainly works of history. Two antagonistic themes run through these histories: *authority*, especially the hierarchically imposed order of monarchical rule, and *liberty*, the free delegation of governmental authority from below, expressing a democratic sentiment. The concept of 'mixed government' celebrated in the 'matchless constitution' is one expression of their reconciliation. More often these two themes conflict, with constitutional development driven by the struggle between them. The longest-standing expression of this conflict occurs in accounts of the feudal order and the ancient constitution or, more lyrically, between the Norman Yoke and the Gothic Bequest.

The Norman Yoke and the Gothic Bequest

The controversy between feudal order and ancient constitution takes us immediately to the Conquest of 1066. There seems little doubt today that this was indeed a conquest: following successful military invasion, William of Normandy declared the entire land of England to be royal property and, after retaining almost 20 per cent himself, proceeded to reward his chief vassals with estates amounting to around 40 per cent of the land. The Normans asserted their sovereign power with a monarchical display of top-down authority, imposing a hierarchy of feudal law on the English.

This account was vigorously contested during the early 17th century by Sir Edward Coke, Chief Justice of the King's Bench and later a leading parliamentarian. In his *Institutes of the Laws of England* (1628–44), Coke conferred judicial authority on the doctrine of the ancient constitution and the immemorial common law. Arguing that the common law is a body of unchanging custom that exists 'time out of the mind of man', Coke maintained that William may have vindicated his claim in trial by battle but he took the throne of England subject to those ancient laws. The common law, Coke claimed, constituted a body of fundamental law that bound both king and subjects.

Coke's reasoning formed one strand of a broader political argument that ancient English liberties were a bequest from the early Saxons, or Goths as they were then called. Their governing arrangements, the argument ran, amounted to an ancient, pre-feudal, and law-observing constitution that preserved liberty. At its core was the great meeting, the *Witenagemote*, where freeborn Anglo-Saxons met to make law and deliberate over the affairs of the kingdom. As Montesquieu later put it: 'the English have taken their idea of political government from the Germans. This fine system was found in the forests.'

The claim that the English had an ancient Gothic constitution has since been widely invoked for political purposes. Arguing that 1066 marked no decisive break in legal continuity, advocates of the Gothic constitution reject the Norman claim of sovereignty. Kings of England, including William I, occupied an office of limited authority and ruled according to the ancient fundamental laws of the land. Their argument also challenges the standard historical account that Parliament came into existence only in the latter half of the 13th century as an instrument of Norman policy. According to the Gothic narrative, the rights of the Commons derive from the ancient *Witenagemote*: the rights of 'freeborn Englishmen' to meet in Parliament derive directly from the ancient constitution, independent of any sanction by kings.

The Gothic narrative is also expressed in the idea of 'the Norman Yoke'. By imposing an alien feudalism on the pre-existing liberty-preserving structure of English government, the Normans corrupted the purity of the ancient Anglo-Saxon constitution. This claim gave rise to a peculiar form of constitutional reasoning: that all political struggles for liberty were really appeals for the restoration of ancient, immemorial liberties. In this light, the great constitutional documents of Magna Carta (1215), the Petition of Right (1628), and the Bill of Rights (1689) did not enact anything new. 'In all our great political struggles', proclaimed the 19th-century constitutional historian E. A. Freeman, 'the voice of the Englishman has never called for the assertion of new principles, for the enactment of new laws; the cry has always been for the better observance of the laws which were already in force, for the redress of grievances which had arisen from their corruption or neglect.' English constitutional development, it was asserted, is marked by the degree to which these ancient liberties—real or imagined—have been restored.

During the conflicts of the 17th century, these competing narratives formed part of the ideological weaponry of royalist and parliamentary forces. Stuart kings proclaimed the absolute character of their prerogative powers to rule. Parliamentary lobbies, by contrast, drew on the Gothic claim, arguing that the true source of governmental power lay with 'the people' as expressed by their representatives in Parliament. With royalists maintaining that Parliament was convened and dissolved according to the king's will and parliamentarians claiming that the Commons alone was the repository of governmental authority, conflict was strained to breaking point. Failure to resolve this through political accommodation led to the dramatic events of the mid-century: civil war, defeat of the royalist cause, execution of the king, formation of the Commonwealth and Protectorate, and then, in 1660, restoration of the monarchy.

These events had a major impact on the shape of the modern British constitution. The modern constitution came into being after the Revolution of 1688 when, once James II had fled the kingdom, a convention Parliament—formed without any king to convene it—offered the throne to William and Mary on terms laid down in the Bill of Rights. The legacy is ambivalent. The upheavals had been literally revolutionary in having gone round full circle and back to a monarchical arrangement. But because of this rotation, the legitimizing principles of modern constitutional government were ambiguous. Was the king above the three estates of lords, bishops, and commons as the law of the constitution stated? Should the king be treated as one of three equal component parts of the sovereign Parliament (king, lords, and commons), as the emerging doctrine of parliamentary sovereignty implied? Should the commons, as sole representative voice of the people, now be accorded clear primacy in the constitution, as the emerging principle of popular sovereignty suggested? These were questions that had to be fudged both to maintain the stability of the post-1688 state and to strengthen the authority of its governing institutions. The modern settlement was marked from the outset by a reluctance to avoid any close examination of its founding principles.

This characteristic of post-1688 constitutional writing shaped a distinctively English style of constitutional scholarship, later called the Whig interpretation of history. The 19th-century Whig historians conceived the English constitution as an elaborate cultural heritage whose study provided a boundless source of prescriptive wisdom. It was the story of the triumph of liberty over absolute sovereign power, evidenced by the increasing importance of representative institutions in the British system. Their work defended such ambiguity as existed, something which manifested itself in distaste for lawyers' approach to the subject.

Constitutional history, they complained, had been perverted by lawyers. This was because 'the legal mind' is congenitally unable to grasp ambiguity, uncertainty, or heterogeneity and is therefore incapable of sensitive historical understanding. This intellectual defect was linked to a political deficiency. Constantly deferring to authority, the natural tendency of the legal mind is conservative. A lack of mental subtlety together with a conservative temperament rendered any lawyer's account of the constitution altogether deficient. The concept of sovereignty, they complained, was a lawyer's invention, nowhere to be found in the historical records. And the main culprit was the 18th-century lawyer Sir William Blackstone.

Blackstone's *Commentaries*

Appointed to the newly established chair in English Law at Oxford, Blackstone wrote the first modern account of the laws of England. His *Commentaries on the Laws of England* (1765–9) was a runaway success, not only in England but throughout the Empire and especially in British North America, where it provided lawyers and judges with an authoritative text in lieu of the practical experience acquired at the Inns of Court in London. Blackstone wrote the work specifically to educate 'the guardians of the English constitution: the makers, repealers, and interpreters of the English laws'. In this he certainly succeeded. The *Commentaries* became the most influential 18th-century account of English/British constitutional law.

The *Commentaries* pioneered the teaching of basic principles of common law, as distinct from canon law and Roman law, as part of university study. It presented the entire body of English law as a system of national law. Since it was commonly believed that the main supporters of royal absolutism were civil lawyers (scholars of Roman law), this initiative enhanced the scholarly status of the indigenous liberty-protecting common law. Blackstone argued that the common law was uniquely English and superior to all other types of law. The *Commentaries* did much to bolster the emerging ideology of nationalism.

Blackstone viewed English constitutional history in the conventional terms of Whig history as the 'gradual restoration of that ancient constitution whereof our Saxon forefathers had been unjustly deprived, partly by the policy and partly by the force, of the Norman'. But—and this is where he parted company with

Whig historians—he also saw the necessity for an absolute central power.

Recognizing that the king's prerogative powers were subject to law, Blackstone nevertheless noted that after 1688 most of these powers had been retained and that the king must be given wide latitude in their manner of exercise. Being 'out of the ordinary course of the common law', these prerogative powers were special and must be treated delicately and deferentially. This was so because the law of the constitution, as distinct from its practice, still 'ascribes to the king, in his high political character... attributes of a great and transcendent nature'. In law, the king was not simply the chief but the sole magistrate of the nation, since all other government officials acted by virtue of his commission. No court could have jurisdiction over the king.

But Blackstone skirted round constitutional fundamentals. Maintaining that the basic legal principle of the constitution was that of the sovereign authority of parliament, for example, he explained that here 'parliament' did not mean the people's representatives in the Commons. It was a purely legal concept, the king convening the three estates of the realm. This is the Crown-in-Parliament: far from being an expression of democratic or popular sentiment, it is a formal expression of state sovereignty.

Blackstone emphasized that the Crown-in-Parliament signified 'that absolute despotic power, which must in all governments reside somewhere, is entrusted by the constitution of these kingdoms'. Its authority knows no limits:

> It can regulate or new model the succession to the crown; as was done in the reign of Henry VIII and William III. It can alter the established religion of the land; as was done in a variety of instances, in the reigns of king Henry VIII and his three children. It can change and create afresh *even the constitution of the kingdom* and of parliaments themselves; as was done by the act of union, and

the several statutes for triennial and septennial elections. It can, in short, do everything that is not naturally impossible.

Since there are no limitations on the authority of this institution, the fundamental rule of the constitution might be reduced to a single sentence: what the Crown-in-Parliament enacts is law.

In this legal analysis, Blackstone downplayed the checks and balances of the three components of Parliament in favour of the conceptual unity of the Crown-in-Parliament. Rather than exalting the authority of the common law as immemorial custom—and therefore as 'fundamental law'—he presented law as a simple positive entity: the commands of the Crown-in-Parliament.

Dicey on the *Law of the Constitution*

During the late 18th and early 19th centuries, Jeremy Bentham and his utilitarian disciples made a sustained attempt to remove the taints of Toryism, Anglicanism, and natural law from Blackstone's account of the constitution. The most influential outcome was A. V. Dicey's *Lectures on the Law of the Constitution* first published in 1885. Dicey, successor to Blackstone at Oxford, was the first to examine the British constitution using an analytical legal method.

He began by both criticizing the formalism of Blackstone and castigating those who promote the virtues of the ancient Gothic constitution and the Whig interpretation of history. The former gave a skewed version of constitutional law, while the latter amounted to 'simple antiquarianism'. His main aim was to rescue the constitution from the historians' grasp and to lay bare its legal fundamentals.

An exponent of analytical legal positivism, Dicey believed that the duty of an English professor of law is simply 'to state what are the laws which form part of the constitution, to arrange them in their order, to explain their meaning, and to exhibit where possible their logical connection'. Constitutional law is concisely defined as 'all rules which directly or indirectly affect the distribution or the exercise of the sovereign power of the state'. These are the rules which define the members of the sovereign power, regulate their relations, and determine the mode through which sovereign power is exercised. The significant word is 'rules'. Dicey uses that term rather than 'laws' so as to divide rules into two types: laws in the strict sense, enforced by the courts, and conventions defined as 'understandings, habits or practices' which, though they regulate the conduct of members of the sovereign power, are not enforceable in courts.

With this simple and elegant approach, Dicey was able to explain the constitution as an assemblage of rules. His method placed the constitutional lawyer at the centre of constitutional scholarship. Rather than venerating the constitution, lawyers must analyse its basic precepts and search for 'the guidance of first principles'. Dicey identified three such principles: the legislative sovereignty of the Crown-in-Parliament, the universal rule throughout the constitution of ordinary law (the 'rule of law'), and the role of constitutional conventions in ordering the constitution. *The Law of the Constitution* sought to explicate these principles and demonstrate their interdependence.

Dicey defines the principle of legislative sovereignty both positively and negatively. It means that 'under the English constitution' the Crown-in-Parliament has 'the right to make or unmake any law whatsoever'. There could be no limitation on legislative competence and no special laws—such as constitutional laws—protected from repeal or amendment. It follows that no institution has the right to set aside the legislation of Parliament; the judiciary must give full and faithful effect to this legislation. He expresses no interest in the 'speculative difficulties' of trying to identify possible limits to this power, simply following Blackstone in maintaining that supreme legislative authority 'must exist in every civilised state'.

Dicey's first principle is a principle of *authority*. But he recognizes that it meshes with the second principle of the constitution—that of the rule of law—to promote *liberty*. Parliamentary sovereignty promotes the 'supremacy of law' because Parliament's commands 'can be uttered only through the combined actions of its three constituent parts', creating a rigid legality that restricts the actions of the executive. For Dicey, the 'rule of law' means the 'absolute supremacy... of regular law as opposed to the influence of arbitrary power'. This rests on a principle of equality before the law, of 'the equal subjection of all classes to the ordinary law of the land administered by the ordinary Law Courts'.

Yet these two constitutional principles do not exist in harmony. Assume, for example, that Parliament enacts a statute that states: 'The Secretary of State may make an order to hold any person whose detention appears to her to be expedient in the interests of the public safety or security of the realm.' If you are dragged from your bed in the middle of the night by police officers enforcing a properly drafted order and then detained for an indefinite period without any explanation other than the Minister's word, you might feel that, even if this executive action is valid according to the principle of legislative sovereignty, it could scarcely be said to comply with the principle of the rule of law. How can these two principles be reconciled?

The answer, Dicey suggests, is found in the third principle: the role of constitutional conventions. Harmony between the first two principles is realized through the working practices of the British constitution. These practices—precepts of political morality which Dicey calls 'constitutional conventions'—ensure that the laws of the constitution are exercised in accordance with a spirit of liberty. These conventional rules regulate the constituent parts of Parliament, ensuring the accountability of the executive to

Parliament, and of Parliament to the public. Dicey's account rests on a delicate set of balances operating within these parliamentary mechanisms.

Bagehot on *The English Constitution*

If Dicey founded the scholarly discipline of British constitutional law, then Walter Bagehot provided the basis for the political scientist's account of the constitution. In *The English Constitution* (1867), Bagehot sought to rescue the constitution from the hands of lawyers by challenging two erroneous interpretations. The first is the separation of powers, a doctrine propounded by Montesquieu with respect to the British constitution and which Blackstone had plagiarized. The second is the idea that British government operated through some Diceyan balance between monarchy, aristocracy, and commons.

Central to Bagehot's method is the distinction between the 'dignified' and the 'efficient' versions of the constitution. The dignified version focuses on the ancient, complex, and ceremonial aspects of the constitution. These 'excite and preserve the reverence of the population' and generate 'its motive power'. The efficient version focuses on the modern, simple, and functional aspects. Deploying that power, these are the parts 'by which it, in fact, works and rules'.

Bagehot's distinction explains how a modern system of government could evolve within the shell of an ancient constitution. The dignified version, 'august with the Gothic grandeur of a more imposing age', exerts its 'imaginative attraction upon an uncultured and rude population' while permitting the sophisticated practices of party politics and parliamentary government to emerge in its shadows. An ancient constitution, he observes, is 'like an old man who still wears with attached fondness clothes in the fashion of his youth: what you see of him is the same; what you do not see is wholly altered'. In this way, the

British state maintains the outer trappings of a monarchy, while becoming a 'disguised republic'.

The symbolism of the queen, Bagehot contends, is incalculable. The monarch offers a visible symbol of unity and strengthens government with the power of religion. Her greatest function is to shroud in mystery the real workings of modern government. Only by maintaining this façade can the idea of a separation of powers between the queen's government, the Parliament, and the judiciary be preserved or the imagery of balance between monarchy, aristocracy, and commons be retained. Far from being based on separation or balance, however, the constitution works through 'the close union, the nearly complete fusion of the executive and legislative powers'. This is its 'efficient secret', at the core of which is the institution of the Cabinet, a committee unknown to law but which, being 'a committee of the legislative body selected to be the executive body', is the most powerful institution in the British system.

Bagehot's book warns against any account of the British constitution that separates law from practice or forms from actuality. The monarch might be the head of the constitution in its dignified version, but the Prime Minister rules according to the efficient. The monarch might be, in Blackstone's words, 'the fountain of honour', but the Treasury is 'the spring of business'. The crown maintains a symbol of unity, but the system of government works through disciplined party division.
The forms suggest separation, but the practice reveals layers of connections.

Bagehot was the last of the great Whig writers. Written on the eve of the second Reform Act, his work expressed mid-Victorian anxieties about the coming of democracy. He believed the country would be unable to make the transition to democracy without maintaining a 'theatrical show' inspiring deference amongst the multitude and bolstering the aristocratic character of the traditional constitution. He was not optimistic. The coming of democracy might not lead, as in France, to the guillotine, but he believed it would lead to the rule of money, especially of 'new money working upon ignorance for its own ends'. Democracy would not come about by sudden revolution, but it would just as surely impair the constitution, and it would do this by 'spoiling our Parliament'.

Twentieth-century constitutional writing

Before the 20th century, constitutional commentary was written exclusively for the edification of the governing class. The proper functioning of the Victorian constitution depended on what Bagehot called the 'upper ten thousand', those 'persons and families possessed of equal culture, and equal faculties, and equal spirit'. This functioning was enhanced by education in a common tradition of conduct, which is why Gladstone believed that 'the public schools of England are part of the constitution'. Bagehot called this arrangement, resting on the high degree of trust in those who exercise power, one of 'club government'. It worked because all public officials—Ministers, parliamentarians, judges, and civil servants—had internalized a common, though implicit, code of conduct.

The most profound change in the early 20th century was the arrival of democracy, with universal adult suffrage finally being achieved in 1928. Democracy brought the Labour party to prominence as parliamentary representatives of the working class, swiftly replacing the Liberals in a two-party system organized around Government and Opposition. Representative democracy produced significant changes in political behaviour, signalled by the institutionalization of ideological politics—the politics of programme, manifesto, and rule book, whether based on Bentham, Marx, or Hayek—and by the emergence of party discipline as a key determinant of political conduct. It also led to unprecedented growth in the powers of government, with government assuming responsibility both for the management of the economy and the welfare of citizens.

Yet these dramatic shifts in government and politics generated little constitutional debate. Warnings were periodically issued about the dangers posed by unchecked growth in the administrative powers of government, most stridently in Chief Justice Hewart's contention in 1929 that Britain was on the brink of a 'new despotism'. But given the nature of the constitution, it was difficult to disentangle constitutional threats from political disputes. And political parties seemed more interested in winning elections than debating constitutional questions. The problem for the Conservatives was that Dicey's principle of the rule of law—especially its incompatibility with the existence of executive discretionary powers—was patently unrealistic, and Conservatives were nothing if not realistic. The challenge facing Labour, by contrast, was not to reform the constitution but to transform society, and the powers bequeathed to government in Bagehot's efficient version of the constitution seemed well suited to the task.

Consequently, until the closing decades of the 20th century there was a remarkable dearth of writing about the constitution. Dicey's conservative assumptions in the *Law of the Constitution* had been challenged from the left by Ivor Jennings's *Law and the Constitution* (1933), but both recognized—notwithstanding their varying use of conjunctions—that *constitution* and *law* were distinct entities. Lawyers gradually became more comfortable in writing about 'constitutional law', but since this is not a technical term of English law its usage is largely a matter of convenience and taste. Without an authoritative legal framework, constitutional lawyers were drawn to descriptive and analytical studies of the principal institutions of government, exemplified in the work of Jennings himself, with his books on *Cabinet Government* (1936), *Parliament* (1939), and *Local Government in the Modern Constitution* (1933). This working method reinforced the conviction that the constitution was merely an object of description, illustrated by Jennings's observation in 1936 that 'the British constitution is changing so rapidly that it is difficult to keep pace with it'. We certainly find nothing in legal scholarship analogous to the normative frameworks of constitutional treatises written by jurists working in regimes with modern constitutions.

This type of institutional analysis did not change once university politics departments had been established. Even more than lawyers, political scientists concentrated on studying the institutions of government to the neglect of constitutional reflection. Knowledge of the British system of government was enhanced by studies of the Cabinet, central and local government, national industries, Parliament, and political parties. But the concern was mainly with efficiency rather than constitutional propriety. In *The British Cabinet* (1962), J. P. Mackintosh criticized the tendency to confer authority on a certain pattern of British government 'based on a simplified version of what did take place in the last third of the nineteenth century'. In reality, 'all of our institutions change as British society and world conditions alter'. It wasn't surprising, therefore, that in the following year John Griffith quipped that 'the constitution is what happens'.

From the mid-1970s, however, the tone began to change. Concerns about economic decline and government overload caused political scientists to engage in more critical examination of the effectiveness of the British system of government. Reflections on 'the state of the nation' led to speculation that perhaps the difficulties were not only economic and political: they might also be constitutional. An early illustration is Nevil Johnson's *In Search of the Constitution* (1977) which advanced the thesis that the constitutional dimension to the British disease manifested itself in 'the atrophy of any language in which we can talk of constitutional issues, of rules, or of principles of public law'. Arguing that the traditional language of the British constitution had lost its ability to sustain authority, Johnson contended that 'we are left floundering in a world of pure pragmatism'. Bagehot might have correctly distinguished between dignified and efficient versions of the constitution but his concern to describe reality caused him to treat the constitution merely as a mechanism and his followers have often overlooked the need to explain its operative values and principles.

From the 1980s onwards, concerns about values and principles became a new orthodoxy. It has since become almost impossible to write about the British constitution without explicitly advocating the need for reform.

Codifying conventions: a twenty-first century theme

One strand of this new orthodoxy is the call to codify the constitution. Various exercises have been undertaken, most notably in the 2014 Report of the House of Commons Political and Constitutional Affairs Committee which outlined a draft written constitution. But this type of exercise has made no political headway. The 1997 Labour government committed to a major programme of constitutional modernization but showed no interest in producing a systematic codification of the existing constitutional rules. And though the Conservative government's December 2019 election manifesto pledged to establish a Constitution, Democracy and Rights Commission, this commitment was never fully realized.

Yet something new has occurred in the last thirty years: the growing conviction that the unwritten rules of constitutional practice must now be formalized. There have always been moments in history when it has been politic to incorporate a conventional understanding in parliamentary statute. The restrictions on prerogative powers in the Bill of Rights of 1689, the position of the House of Lords with respect to money bills in the Parliament Act 1911, the relationship between Parliament and the Dominions in the Statute of Westminster 1931 are all illustrations of such moments. But these were markers of progressive evolutionary change. The current initiative reflects the conviction that, despite embodying important values, constitutional conventions no longer have authority unless they are produced in written form.

The recent move to convert conventions into a series of formal rule books has been driven by the serious decline in standards of political conduct. One catalyst was the 1990s scandal of MPs accepting cash for asking parliamentary questions. This caused the government to establish the *Committee on Standards in Public Life*, which recommended that all public bodies adopt formal codes of conduct expressing seven basic principles of public life: selflessness, integrity, objectivity, accountability, openness, honesty, and leadership.

The enhanced standing of such codes is illustrated by changes in the status of another document, the *Ministerial Code*. The origins of the Ministerial Code lie in a Cabinet Paper, *Questions of Procedure for Ministers*, first issued by Prime Minister Attlee in 1945. This confidential document laid down general guidelines of ministerial conduct distilled from precedents of previous administrations. It was reproduced in amended form for all post-war governments, but the document was only declassified in 1992. At first merely 'tips on etiquette', it has evolved into an elaborate code of conduct for Ministers covering potential conflict between public duties and private interests, ministerial and parliamentary responsibilities, and governmental and party roles. In 1996, the Ministerial Code was complemented by the publication of a *Civil Service Code* which in 2010 was put onto a statutory foundation. And in 2011 the government published the *Cabinet Manual*, a 110-page document providing 'a source of information on the laws, conventions and rules that affect the operation and procedures of the Government'.

In a break with the traditional understanding of Parliament as a self-regulating institution, the Standards Committee also proposed a new Code of Conduct for MPs to be overseen by an Independent Parliamentary Commissioner for Standards. And in the wake of the MPs' expenses scandal in 2009, this new regime was further extended. MPs could no longer set their own expenses regime, a task that was transferred to a new Independent Parliamentary Standards Authority equipped with statutory authority to draft and police the new rules.

The relentless conversion of 'tacit understandings' into formal rule books indicates the extent to which the British constitution is now in fact written. The challenge today no longer concerns a lack of clarity about standards: it is about their enforceability. Consider, for example, the codification in the Scotland Act 2016 of the convention that Westminster will not generally legislate for devolved matters without the consent of the devolved legislature. When the Scottish government sought to enforce this principle by judicial review of the UK government's decision to trigger exit from the European Union, the Supreme Court held that the courts are 'neither the parents nor the guardians of political conventions; they are merely observers'. Despite being promulgated in a statute, enforcement of the convention 'does not lie within the constitutional remit of the judiciary'.

Left to the government, these rules are prey to party considerations. When in 2021 Owen Paterson MP was found to have breached standards on paid lobbying, the government sought to avoid a parliamentary vote sanctioning a former Conservative minister by changing the rules on standards. Enforceability has also been the most contentious aspect of recent breaches of the Ministerial Code. In 2020, an inquiry by the government's independent adviser on the Code concluded that Priti Patel, the then Home Secretary, had breached the Code by bullying civil servants, but the Prime Minister refused to take any action. This led to the adviser's resignation, and a subsequent judicial review also failed, with the court holding that the PM was the ultimate arbiter of the Code.

The most egregious aspect of rule enforcement, however, concerns breaches of Coronavirus lockdown regulations in Downing Street. The 2020–2 pandemic caused the government, with minimal parliamentary oversight, to impose the most stringent restrictions on personal freedom ever effected in peacetime history. But despite the rhetoric that 'we're all in this together', it later emerged that throughout 2021 a series of parties in breach of the regulations had been held in Downing Street. In December 2021, Prime Minister Johnson had stated in Parliament that 'the guidance was followed and the rules were followed at all times'. But a subsequent police investigation led to more than one hundred fines being issued, including to the PM, his wife, the Chancellor of the Exchequer, and senior government officials. An inquiry by civil servant Sue Gray concluded that these events stemmed from a failure of leadership, both political and official. These reports provide evidence that the PM had acted in breach of all seven principles of public life, but he nonetheless avoided the sanction of being forced to resign. Until, that is, a remarkable episode when, in a period of less than 48 hours over 6–7 July 2022, over 50 MPs resigned their governmental posts following the revelation that the PM had ignored warnings of sexual misconduct by the Deputy Chief Whip. This left Johnson with no alternative.

In his preface to the 2019 version of the Ministerial Code, Johnson had stated that 'to win back the trust of the British people, we must uphold the very highest standards of propriety—and this code sets out how we must do so'. He explained that there must be 'no bullying' and the 'precious principles of public life enshrined in this document…must be honoured at all times'. The Code, he continued, recognizes the 'overarching duty on Ministers to comply with the law' and emphasizes the 'paramount importance that

1. 'And what's going on here? Looks like you've arranged to meet someone from a different household!'

Ministers give accurate and truthful information to Parliament, correcting any inadvertent error at the earliest opportunity'. Ministers who knowingly mislead Parliament 'will be expected' to resign. The performance of the Johnson administration offers compelling evidence that, notwithstanding the conversion of tacit understandings into formal rules, the efficacy of those rules depends on party political considerations. Following his resignation as PM in June 2022, Johnson resigned as an MP twelve months later. This followed a report from the House of Commons Privileges Committee which held that he had committed a serious contempt in deliberately misleading Parliament when stating that the guidance had at all times been followed.

In further revisions to the Code in May 2022, the government emphasized that it would not be appropriate to put the Code on a legislative foundation because 'this would undermine the constitutional settlement by conflating the executive and legislature, and would provide an additional route where the judiciary may also be drawn into such (political) matters that the Government considers to be non-justiciable'. That statement may be correct but it does nothing to mitigate the point that without the internal acceptance of these standards by all officials, formal promulgation is of merely symbolic value.

Chapter 4
Parliamentary government

Parliament: the mirror of the nation

The most distinctive features of the British constitution are its arrangements for parliamentary government. Britain made an evolutionary, not revolutionary, transition to modernity and this is attributable to the flexibility of those practices. But parliamentary government is misunderstood if, as often happens today, these practices are made to fit a template of modern constitutionalism and Parliament's role limited to that of a legislature. The peculiar strength of parliamentary government lies in the complexity and ambiguity of its institutional arrangements and in the confluence rather than separation of governing tasks.

Since its formation in the late 13th century, the tasks assumed by Parliament have varied considerably. At times an opposition to the overweening power of government, Parliament has also been deployed as a powerful instrument of government. Often portrayed as a beacon of liberal democracy, Parliament has at critical moments been the tool of monarchy and oligarchy. Presenting itself as a legislature, Parliament has also assumed roles as a council and a court. And its survival over time owes as much to its weakness and mutability as to its strength.

Parliament's continued existence is the single most important indicator of the character of Britain's evolutionary constitution. Parliament was the primary means through which the English forged both a sense of political unity and a national identity. To an unusual extent, Parliament came to symbolize the 'political nation'. Its central place in the practice of governing is the main reason why the British have never devised a legal concept of the state or, until recently, established a system of administrative law. Parliament holds the key to understanding the peculiar character of both the British constitution and the British state.

The main objectives of this chapter are to explain how Parliament acquired its status as the 'mirror of the nation', to assess its role today, and to consider how far its current standing reflects dissatisfaction with the British constitution. The practices of parliamentary government come out of a rich history of struggle between the crown and the communities of the realm, with the crown holding on to its prerogatives of governing against those who, in the name of liberty, sought to limit those powers within fixed institutional forms. This struggle led to the emergence of a composite sovereign authority, that of the Crown-in-Parliament. But this was achieved only after civil war (1642–9), the execution of Charles I (1649), the formation of the Commonwealth and Protectorate (1649–60), the restoration of the king (1660), and a revolution which led to the removal of James II and, at the instigation of a convention Parliament, the crowning of William and Mary (1688). Only after the Revolution of 1688 and the formation of a British state after 1707 did conditions exist for the emergence of an abstract concept of parliamentary sovereignty.

Origins of Parliament

Parliament's origins lie in late 13th-century political developments. The Norman Conquest had produced a unified and highly centralized kingdom, ensuring that the political feudalism characteristic of many European kingdoms—in which the king had to negotiate with powerful barons—could not develop. A strong monarchy was quickly established, carrying the danger that this monarchical power might be abused.

This threat materialized in the late 12th century as the Angevin kings sought to use their powerbase in England to expand their continental empire. After a series of disastrous and expensive wars in which King John lost Normandy in 1204 and suffered defeats in Flanders and France in 1214, the barons struck back. Challenging the system of Norman government that had been constructed over the previous 150 years, they required the king to grant a charter of liberties. This was the Magna Carta of 1215.

Magna Carta was not some great work of the 'nation' or the 'people', as the Whig constitutional historians were later to claim. The barons asserted their authority primarily by requiring the king to govern through a council, establishing the principle that acts of the king had an official character. The subsequent history of this relationship is messy with no consistent legal differentiation between king and crown. But it is from the concept of the crown—the king in his official capacity—that our understanding of government evolves. The great significance of Magna Carta—in contrast to similar charters negotiated throughout continental Europe during this period—is that, whereas the demand for liberties on the Continent led to barons obtaining independence within their fiefdoms, the objective of the English barons had been to acquire a share in an already well-established centralized system of government.

Magna Carta required that no taxes be levied 'except by the common counsel of our realm'. During the reign of Henry III (1216–72) the meeting of king in council was the form through which the 'community of the realm' expressed its will. By the mid-13th century, however, Henry had started to require each of the shires to send two knights to supplement the work of the council. This was the precedent for the formation of Parliament.

2. 'You can read, right?—I want you to check this thing for loopholes'

Parliament was consolidated during the 14th century as it became convenient to amalgamate the *estates*, the meeting with tenants-in-chief to discuss financial necessities, with *parlement*, the hearing of petitions in cases referred by the king's judges. It is in this latter sense that we trace Parliament's origins back to a high court. But only at the end of Edward III's long reign (1327–77) was Parliament transformed from an event into an institution. This was driven by financial necessity: the need for revenues to meet the cost of the wars in France and Scotland.

The institution forged during this period acquired its strength from three sources. First, Parliament was formed from the union between a high court of justice and a body (the estates) charged with taxing and representative responsibilities. Once it was recognized that individual petitions contained common grievances, Parliament's role changed from a court into a more general governmental forum. Secondly, Parliament was a forum in which the council, the coordinating agent of the king's government, controlled the agenda. If Parliament had been simply a body that checked the crown, it would have withered; its survival depended on its usefulness as an instrument of royal government. Thirdly, its mode of representation, which required attendance not just from the barons but also two representatives from each of the shires, ensured that the decisions of the 'knights of the shires' bound their constituents. Representation was not experienced as the expression of democratic sentiment. Instead it was seen as a form of feudal service which bound local communities.

The English Parliament that evolved during the later Middle Ages came into being as an act of royal will. But it is something of a stretch to claim continuity with the Anglo-Saxon *Witenagemote*. Often presented as an institution to counterbalance government, in fact the origins of Parliament lie in its value to the king in the business of governing. The great strength of this arrangement lay in the fact that the king's court, the king's council, and the king's Parliament together formed an elaborate system of multi-layered government. Integration rather than separation strengthened the structure. But there was an even more enduring legacy: the continued existence of Parliament ensured that a national system of government would be established on something deeper and broader than monarchical authority.

Parliament and the formation of the state

Parliamentary assemblies were a common feature of early 16th-century European regimes. Nevertheless, by the end of the century the English Parliament was one of few representative institutions still in existence. It owed its survival mainly to the use Henry VIII made of it during the upheavals of the Reformation.

The great Reformation Parliament summoned by Henry in 1529 lasted for nearly seven years. Henry made full use of the authority of the Crown-in-Parliament, not only to eliminate medieval privileges encumbering the exercise of his authority, most of which belonged to the Church, but also to effect a revolutionary break with the Church in Rome. Crown and Parliament united to challenge rival jurisdictions. As Henry stated in a speech to Parliament in 1543, 'we at no time stand so highly in our estate royal as in the time of Parliament; wherein we as head and you as members are conjoined and knit together into one body politic'. Parliament became a key component of Tudor statecraft.

There was now no limitation on what the Crown-in-Parliament could determine. By legislative action, the Church was placed under the authority of the king, changing the established religion of the land. When Henry's offspring later sought to advance (Edward VI), reverse (Mary), or reintroduce the reforms (Elizabeth I) they could do so only by introducing new legislation in Parliament. The Act of Parliament had become the highest expression of law. These actions substantially enhanced the authority of the House of Commons, which by the end of the 16th century had emerged as an independent body protective of its own privileges. When the Stuart kings tried to rule more informally, asserting their divine right, the stage was set for confrontation between the 'head' and the 'members' of this 'one body politic'.

Parliament initially responded to these informal methods of governing by reviving the power of impeachment. Since it was accepted that 'the king can do no wrong', any wrongfulness in government had to be attributed to the 'evil counsel' of his Ministers. Punishment for such evil counsel was enforced by the parliamentary procedure of impeachment. Impeachment actions against such leading Ministers as Sir Francis Bacon (1621), the Duke of Buckingham (1626–8), and the Earl of Strafford (1640–1) heightened the tensions between king and Parliament. By punishing the king's agents, Parliament was presuming to understand the public good better than the king himself.

In 1629, Charles I's solution was to dissolve Parliament and rule without it for the next eleven years. But he was forced to summon a Parliament in 1640, as he was desperate for additional revenue to raise an army against the rebellious Scots. At this point, Parliament acted decisively to set terms for the redress of grievances, laid down as Nineteen Propositions. The king's rejection of them on the ground that they would lead to the destruction of the 'mixed constitution' caused the country to drift into civil war. It was during this period that parliamentarians began to state clearly that the true source of governmental power lay not in God, nor in the king as God's vicegerent on earth, but in the people. Under the English constitution that power was located in the Commons. Having come into existence as an act of royal will, Parliament—invoking the principle of popular sovereignty—now assumed the power of self-creation.

Parliamentary forces eventually claimed victory in the civil war and Charles was placed on trial. His defence that 'the king can do no wrong' being rejected, he was found guilty of treason and in January 1649 was executed. England became a republic and the office of the king—along with the House of Lords and the established (Anglican) Church—was abolished. Parliament remained in existence as the formal locus of authority, but in reality power was held by the army. In 1653, the army effectively seized control, Oliver Cromwell was proclaimed Lord Protector, and the Instrument of Government—England's first and only written constitution—was drafted. But as the Puritan revolution unravelled, Parliament was dissolved in 1658 and then, after the death of Cromwell, in 1660 the monarchy—along with Parliament and the Church—was restored.

With the restoration of the monarchy under Charles II, son of the executed king, attempts were made to redefine the balance between the crown and Parliament, but many ambiguities remained. When in 1685 Charles was succeeded by his Catholic brother, James II sought to resolve these. His solution was to begin a programme of centralization and modernization modelled on the absolutist French regime of Louis XIV. But James's succession had divided the ruling elite: the Tories supported the principle of 'divine right', while the Whigs wanted to exclude James from the throne. When James proceeded to implement his policies and rule without Parliament, the Whig magnates, fearing a subversion of the constitution, sought help from the Protestant Dutch.

In November 1688, William of Orange—who was married to James's Protestant daughter Mary—landed in England at the head of an army. He pledged to uphold a free Parliament and was willing to negotiate terms enabling James to keep his throne, albeit with reduced powers. But in December James fled the country and the ruling elite determined that he had forfeited the crown. A convention Parliament was held and, in a compromise between adherence to the hereditary principle and 'reason of state' argument, invited William and Mary to reign jointly. This act established the principle that succession to the throne is determined by Act of Parliament.

The modern constitutional settlement

The terms of the constitutional settlement were formally expressed in the Bill of Rights of 1689. This Act affirmed the Protestant character of the English state and, by removing certain of the king's prerogatives, established a constitutional monarchy. More than this: by establishing the principle that prerogative powers could be abolished by Act of Parliament, the Bill of Rights led directly to the legal doctrine of Parliament's absolute legislative authority, underpinned by affirmation of the principle of free and regular Parliaments.

The 1688 Revolution placed the Whig magnates in a powerful position, leading to a period—lasting almost eighty years—of Whig supremacy. In this era of relatively stable aristocratic rule, the main conventions of constitutional government were forged. It was also a time of great economic and social change during which Britain was transformed from an insular society with an agricultural economy to an industrial and commercial nation underpinned by a fiscal-military state of considerable imperial might. These developments are linked: constitutional modernization provided the conditions of political and commercial stability that fuelled the industrial revolution.

Constitutional conflicts of the 17th century had centred on the clash between the crown's divine right to rule and Parliament's claim to be the institution from which the king's government derived its powers. In adopting the composite form of Crown-in-Parliament as the source of authority, the 1689 settlement fudged the finer points of constitutional principle. Practical wisdom had decreed separation between government and legislature. Although government remained in the hands of the king, Parliament possessed the ultimate instruments of control. The formal authority of the king's government was retained but it depended on an institution that presented itself as guardian of civil liberties. The 'matchless constitution' of parliamentary government survived not on the basis of fixed formal principles but on a procedural framework of considerable flexibility.

Consider, for example, the abiding 17th-century concern over standing armies which could be used as instruments of oppression. The Bill of Rights had declared such armies unlawful without the consent of Parliament, but this did not lead to their elimination. On the contrary, between 1680 and 1780 the British army and navy trebled in size. Command of military forces remained part of the crown's prerogative powers, but authority to sanction this growth rested with Parliament. The military thus became a tool of *national* rather than simply *royal* power. The post-1688 settlement did not lead to a reduction in the scale of government: it operated to ensure that Parliament would become a central actor.

The settlement is generally labelled 'representative and responsible government'. Since the policies of the king's government had to be supported by Parliament, the most effective way of achieving this was to appoint parliamentary leaders as the king's Ministers. This led to renewed tensions as the crown used its powers of patronage to seduce leaders from allegiance to their parliamentary parties, and parliamentary parties in turn sought to acquire control over the government. It was a struggle that Parliament eventually won.

In the process, legal methods of ensuring governmental accountability were replaced by political methods. Impeachment fell into disuse when Parliament discovered a more informal but equally effective means of ensuring ministerial accountability: rather than pursuing legal proceedings, Parliament realized that a simple majority vote would suffice to require a Minister to resign. The legal principle that the king could do no wrong was retained only because the king eventually became a cipher, able to act only on the advice of others.

The process of establishing representative and responsible government was quickly consolidated following complications over the royal succession. In the 1689 settlement it was assumed that once James II (in exile) and William III had died, the monarchy would revert to its normal course. This proved ill-founded: following William's death in 1702, Mary's sister, Anne, became queen, but since Anne's last surviving child had died in 1700, the end of the Protestant line seemed imminent. On the hereditary principle, James II's son, Prince James Francis Edward Stuart ('the Old Pretender'), was next in line. Having been raised as a Catholic in France, however, James was entirely unacceptable to the Whig ruling elite. They therefore proposed to settle the line of succession on the Protestant heirs of Sophia, Electress of Hanover and granddaughter of James I. The Act of Settlement 1701 made provision for this, in one stroke putting paid to both divine right and hereditary monarchy.

By the time Prince Georg Ludwig, Sophia's son, assumed the throne in 1714 as George I, his powers had been significantly curtailed. Although the prerogatives of government remained vested in the crown, the king had to appoint Ministers who could manage Parliament and direct the administration. Elevating the Hanoverians accelerated this process. George I took little part in Cabinet meetings. No doubt his lack of English was something of a drawback but what he recognized more fundamentally was his lack of authority.

The constitutional impact was dramatic. Seventeenth-century conflicts between the crown and Parliament were replaced in the 18th century by tensions within Parliament itself. As competing factions vied for control of government, distinct political parties were formed, not as an expression of democracy but as vehicles for managing Parliament. As the emerging Whig and Tory parties became locked in ritualized conflict for control of government, the main practices of modern government—what Dicey later called 'constitutional conventions'—came into being.

The main functions of these constitutional conventions were twofold: first to transfer the exercise of the crown's prerogative powers to representative Ministers; and then to ensure that Ministers remained accountable to Parliament. The conventions of collective responsibility (the constitutional principle upholding Cabinet government) and individual ministerial responsibility (the constitutional principle requiring Ministers to account for all decisions of their departments) became central features of the British constitution. The traditional idea of a balance between monarchy, aristocracy, and commons was replaced by a balance between the parliamentary parties: between HM Government and HM Loyal Opposition.

Democratization

Nations are not primarily ruled by laws, still less by violence, as Burke noted in 1770. They are ruled by knowledge of the temper of a people and judicious management. Since the first duty of a politician must therefore be to understand this temper, Burke opposed the tendency of the crown to run government like a court. This is why he supported the emergence of political parties. A party, he explained, 'is a body of men united for promoting by their joint endeavours the national interest upon some particular principle in which they are all agreed'. Political parties ensure that politicians act in accordance with these principles rather than their private considerations.

But Burke defended aristocratic government: he promoted the case for government of the people and for the people, but not by the people. Reinforcing this in a speech to the electors of Bristol in 1774, he explained that although a representative must listen to the wishes of his constituents, the idea that he would act on instruction or mandate was contrary to the whole tenor of the constitution. Parliament, he elaborated, was not a trading house of competing interests but a deliberative assembly of one nation, with one interest—the national interest. A representative could not sacrifice his judgement to the interests of his constituents but must be guided by the best interests of the nation. Parliament might be, in Coke's words, 'the grand inquest of the nation', but it was an inquest conducted only by our 'betters'.

The political struggles of the late 18th century were dominated by attempts to extend the franchise and reform the corrupt constituency system. This cause was knocked back by British reaction to the violence of the French Revolution, which led to heightened concern about the dangers of tampering with the intricate balances of 'the matchless constitution'. By the early 19th century, however, many felt that this wave of reaction threatened the unity and stability of the British state. Writing in 1831, Hegel had argued that, although the British constitution was to be admired for its achievements in reconciling authority and liberty, its constitutional development had become stultified. This was a direct consequence of its 18th-century achievements. The relative weakness of the monarchy together with the hegemony of the privileged landed class had removed the threat of absolutism, but it was now causing the aristocracy to ignore the interests of unpropertied workers.

This lack of national unity, which Hegel believed only the crown could provide, became a barrier to further evolution. The 18th-century elite might have accepted the principle of Blackstone's argument that the Act of Parliament 'can change and create afresh even the constitution of the kingdom', but it had seen no reason to do so with respect to the franchise. The breakthrough came only with the Reform Act of 1832.

Despite providing only a modest extension of the franchise, the 1832 Act marked the beginning of modern electoral reform. By extending the franchise to just over 5 per cent of the population, it was hardly a great democratizing measure. It nonetheless marked a major constitutional turning point because, as a compromise measure devoid of principle, it paved the way for the gradual democratization of the Commons. The Representation of the People Act 1867, which doubled the size of the electorate, was more radical, but the 1832 Act had established the vital precedent that the franchise could be changed by statute. That the 1867 Act was introduced by a Tory government is significant: having accepted Bagehot's argument about England being a deferential country, the Tories soon came round to the view that they could still win elections on an expanded franchise. Their convictions were later justified by the emergence of Tory working-class voters maintaining loyalty to the crown, which has since become a decisive electoral factor.

After 1867, the struggle to establish universal suffrage was marked by significant reforms in 1884, 1918, and the eventual realization of that goal in 1928. With the establishment of universal adult suffrage came the formation of disciplined political parties: Conservatives, Liberals, and, from the beginning of the 20th century, the Labour party. The growth of class consciousness, however, meant that these parties were perceived as representing sectional interests of society in the Commons. Such ideological divisions meant that the traditional idea of a balanced constitution between monarch, aristocracy, and the people was unsustainable. It was replaced by conflict, with the two hereditary elements of monarchy and aristocracy operating as a brake on the will of the elected chamber.

That conflict came to a head when the House of Lords rejected the Liberal government's budget in 1909. The so-called 'People's Budget' had proposed unprecedented taxes on the wealthy to fund new social programmes. The ensuing constitutional crisis was resolved only after two general elections in 1910: the first to assert the authority of the Commons over the Lords with respect to the budget and the second to assert the authority of the Commons over the king, who had refused to appoint 250 new Liberal peers to remove the inbuilt Conservative majority in the Lords without this again being tested at the polls. When the Liberals won both elections, the Lords reluctantly gave their consent to the Parliament Act 1911.

The 1911 Act removed the House of Lords' veto power. The necessity for their consent to 'money bills' was entirely removed and other Bills approved by the Commons in three successive sessions could receive the Royal Assent without the consent of the Lords, a procedure subsequently reduced to two successive sessions by the Parliament Act of 1949. The Commons was formally recognized as the pivot of modern constitutional government. Paradoxically, this moment of triumph also marked the beginning of the subversion of parliamentary authority. The Lords had rejected the 1909 budget, arguing that it needed to be submitted 'to the judgment of the country'. The 'people' thus made its first formal entry into constitutional discourse.

This principle of popular authority was subsequently generalized by Dicey. In 1914, he argued that 'a not unfairly elected legislature may misrepresent the permanent will of the electors' and might produce 'a machine which may well lead to political corruption'. With the coming of democratic majority government, Dicey, the most authoritative exponent of the legal doctrine of parliamentary sovereignty, started to unpick the logic of his own constitutional argument and to claim that the 'permanent will' of the people expressed in a referendum might possess a higher authority than that of Parliament.

Modern parliamentary practice

In *The English Constitution* (1867), Bagehot had identified five main functions of the House of Commons. The first and most important was to act as an electoral chamber: Parliament 'is the assembly which chooses our president [i.e. the Prime Minister]'. The second was expressive: to express 'the mind of the English people on all matters which come before it'. Third was the educative function, whereby this 'great and open council' must provide leadership and 'teach the nation what it does not know'. Fourthly, it had an informing function, of laying before the crown the grievances and complaints of sections of society. Finally there was the legislative function. Although neglecting the question of supply (i.e. approval of taxation), Bagehot's catalogue provides a useful template for assessing how the role of Parliament has altered since the Victorian era.

Over the last 150 years, government has greatly extended its range, assuming responsibility for improving social conditions by regulating economic activity and providing a wide range of public services. This massive expansion has had a major impact on Parliament's role, as can be gauged by changes since Bagehot's day.

In specifying legislation as the last of his five functions, Bagehot was making a point. In the dignified version of the constitution, Parliament is the supreme, all-powerful legislature. But in the efficient—'what actually happens'—version, Parliament does not play any major role. Since the 19th century, Parliament has rarely had a major impact on the content of legislation. Responsibility for proposing and drafting the vast bulk of legislation rests with the government, which, because of its parliamentary majority, is generally able to have its Bills enacted into law in the desired form. Parliament, it is sometimes argued, does not even engage in effective scrutiny of these Bills. This is partly because of the cumbersome nature both of debating procedures on the floor of the House and of arrangements for the detailed examination of Bills in standing committees. It is partly because of their technical complexity, especially with the current practice of approving only a skeletal framework in primary legislation, with details being delegated to the government to supply by way of executive legislation, such as Statutory Instruments. But it is also because of the sheer volume of legislation, much of it tabled in an unfinished form, which, given the pressures on the parliamentary timetable, provides little time for adequate consideration.

During the 20th century, the number of Bills enacted in a parliamentary session has hardly changed. What has altered dramatically is the length and complexity of this legislation. In 1900, Parliament enacted 63 Acts amounting to fewer than 200 pages of the statute book. In 1950, only 51 Acts were passed but these took up over 1,000 pages. By 2000, the 45 Acts passed filled nearly 4,000 (larger-sized) pages of the statute book. This is just the tip of the iceberg. The volume of executive legislation passed during the 20th century grew tenfold: from around 300 Statutory Instruments (SIs) of under 1,000 pages in 1900 to 3,500 SIs amounting to over 10,000 pages in 2000.

We get some sense of the scale of the 21st-century problem by considering the two most important challenges recently faced by government: effecting withdrawal from the European Union after 2016 and taking action to deal with Coronavirus from 2020. Both tasks have involved unprecedented use of the powers of delegated legislation. Responding to the pandemic, the government promoted the Coronavirus Act 2020, a measure of 348 pages that completed all its Commons stages in one day and received the royal assent two days later. This primary legislation was followed by far-reaching powers acquired by regulations, many of which were adopted without any prior parliamentary oversight or approval. Far from being technical details, these regulations extended police powers and imposed stringent controls on businesses, on public gatherings, and on freedom of movement in general. And that is not all: Parliament also authorized an unprecedented increase to the government budget, running to hundreds of billions of pounds, without any specific indication of the purposes to which it was to be applied. This enormous governmental programme was run entirely by ministerial decree and with minimal parliamentary oversight. It is often said that, although legislation must be approved by Parliament, it is more accurate to say that Parliament legitimates rather than legislates. But the role of Parliament in the pandemic suggests that even this legitimizing role is now threadbare.

Over the last 150 years, then, legislative and policy action has shifted decisively from parliamentary to governmental processes. This could not have occurred without a major expansion in governmental capacity. In the early 19th century, the Home Secretary was apparently assisted by only two under-secretaries and eighteen clerks. Since then there has been a dramatic increase in administrative capacity. Basic reforms were introduced as a consequence of the Northcote–Trevelyan Report of 1854, which sought to eliminate the link between patronage and the exercise of administrative power by instituting a permanent non-political civil service recruited on merit through competitive examination. The creation of this professional civil service converted the binary separation of power—between government and Parliament—into a tripartite system in which the actions of both government and Parliament are disciplined and checked by the permanent administration of the country.

In the British system, Ministers are burdened with a vast catalogue of responsibilities. These range from initiating legislation and taking it through its parliamentary stages, policy-making, making executive decisions on all issues within their departmental remit, making appointments, handling complaints, managing their departments, and contributing to the formation of collective government policy. None of these tasks could be realized without the civil service. Civil servants ensure the seamless continuity of governmental business throughout changes in Ministries and also—given that their average term in office is only two years—in Ministers. Behind every Minister is his or her alter ego, the official charged with the duty of offering advice and implementing decisions. This is the 'efficient secret' of the contemporary constitution. The British constitution works not merely because of the link between legislature and executive through the Cabinet system but also because of the link between the transient (elected politicians) and the permanent (civil servants) in the running of the machinery of government.

This system is legitimated through the twin conventions of ministerial responsibility. The convention of collective responsibility rests on three main practices: *secrecy*, meaning that government decision-making should take place in private to encourage forthright discussion; *unanimity*, meaning that once a decision is made all members of the government must support it; and *confidence*, meaning that the government must retain the support of Parliament and must resign if it loses a vote of confidence. The convention of individual ministerial responsibility maintains that the Minister must answer publicly—and especially in Parliament—for all decisions of his or her department. The efficacy of these conventions might be doubted, but the extent that they continue to hold authority depends on the workings of the civil service. All government meetings must be held in the presence of officials who minute decisions and maintain records, thereby ensuring clarity, formality, and consistency. Governing with reference to precedents ensures the maintenance of probity and impartiality in the conduct of governmental business. This is bolstered by the convention of civil servant anonymity: to be able to serve all governments faithfully, civil servants should not be identified as playing a role in the shaping and making of governmental decisions.

Collective responsibility brings us back to the first of Bagehot's functions: Parliament's role in determining who will run the government. By convention, the monarch must invite the person best able to form a government that commands the confidence of the Commons. A primary function of Parliament is to identify the Prime Minister and to sustain that person in office, a task now delegated to the intricate workings of the party machines. Party machinery—the Whips' office and shadowy arrangements known as 'the usual channels'—not only controls the agenda of the Commons but also the fate of Ministers and Ministries. These 'efficient' party-controlled operations working through the 'dignified' conventions of responsibility have led many to the conclusion that there has been a 'waning of constitutional understanding': governmental decisions are now made through party mechanisms rather than in accordance with traditional constitutional practice.

This point is exemplified in the role of the Prime Minister. This office is scarcely known to the law of the constitution and is certainly not defined by law. Yet, by combining leadership of the party with leadership of the government machine, it has effectively assumed a new type of monarchical status. Elevation of the office has come about partly through its powers of patronage, such as the appointment and dismissal of Ministers. But it is also the result of the PM's contemporary role as both shaper and barometer of popular opinion. Monarchy is a type of strong government, Bagehot argued, primarily because it is intelligible government. 'The nature of a constitution, the action of an assembly, the play of parties, the unseen formation of a guiding opinion'—all of these, he claimed, are 'complex facts, difficult to know, and easy to mistake'. By contrast, 'the action of a single will, the fiat of a single mind, are easy ideas; anyone can make them out and no one can forget them'. In the modern world, the office of the monarch is subsumed within that of the Prime Minister.

In his introduction to a new edition of Bagehot in 1963, Richard Crossman clarified this shift. He contended that Cabinet government had been relegated to the dignified version of the constitution and replaced by a system of prime ministerial government. Crossman's thesis has since provoked heated debate in which the personality of the PM cannot be discounted. But the general trajectory is clear: Cabinets meet less frequently, for shorter periods, and with fewer papers to consider. Government policy is increasingly made by the Prime Minister in informal, bilateral, and unminuted meetings with Ministers, briefed by special advisers rather than career civil servants. In such a regime, the power of the PM is barely limited if his or her standing in the opinion polls is high. But when those ratings plummet, then, as the experiences of Thatcher, Blair, Brown, May, and Truss illustrate, power dissipates and they become greatly dependent on the support of power-holders within the party.

If Parliament's influence in electing the Prime Minister and making laws has waned, so too has its authority to express the mind of the people and educate the nation. A series of scandals—extending from 'cash for questions' in the 1990s, 'cash for honours' in 2006–7, parliamentary expenses in 2009, sexual misconduct allegations in 2017, and bullying of staff in 2018—has greatly diminished the standing of Parliament in the eyes of the public. Once a jealous protector of its own unique privileges—underpinned by the provision in the Bill of Rights that no proceedings in Parliament can be questioned in any court—it is now subjected to an increasing amount of independent oversight.

Do these developments mean the destruction of the traditional constitution? Before yielding to pessimism, it might be noted that there is one important parliamentary function that Bagehot underplayed: Parliament's role in testing Ministers through debates, questions, and the scrutiny of select committee hearings. This too is under strain, not least because Ministers attend Parliament less frequently. But the power of select committees has recently been enhanced following the Wright Report of 2009 which led to committee members being elected by secret ballots. And it remains the case that, behind the ritualized arrangements of Government and Opposition, Parliament still has an important role in demanding openness in government, in promoting higher standards of ministerial probity and competence, and in maintaining a nursery of ambitious MPs who, through constant testing, acquire the experience needed to become effective Ministers. Whether it can continue to perform this role effectively remains an open question.

Chapter 5
Reconfiguring the state

Modern constitutional democracies commonly have a constitution drafted in the name of 'the people' that establishes a system of government relating to a clearly defined territory. But in the British case, the territory, the people, and the governing principles they are supposed to have authorized are all matters of considerable ambiguity. The reason for this is the nature of the state which has its seat of government in London. This state—the United Kingdom of Great Britain and Northern Ireland—has a complex history.

England, Britain, United Kingdom

As the largest, most powerful nation on the islands, the English have always sought to dominate the Irish, Scots, and Welsh, primarily to maintain the security of their state. After 1066, Wales was incorporated into the English state. This was achieved by a brutal policy of conquest brought to a formal conclusion by the Statute of Wales of 1535 by which Welsh lands were absorbed into the English shire system and the English common law applied throughout England and Wales. The story with respect to the Scots and Irish is more complicated. Throughout modern political history, the Scots and Irish have used—and been used by—other European powers as part of an ongoing island struggle, often tangled up in questions of religious allegiance.

Scotland. The essential point about Anglo-Scottish relations is that the union between the two nations was not forged by conquest but by treaty. In 1707, Scotland and England were joined by the Treaty of Union to create the United Kingdom of Great Britain. This was the culmination of a longer and more complicated process. Lowland Scots, for example, once saw themselves as part of a common Saxon heritage. For them the critical division within Britain was not that between English and Scot, or Saxon and Celt, but between Saxon and Norman. Lowland Scots shared with the English the narrative of maintaining Saxon liberty against the threat of the Norman Yoke. Having little in common with the feudal organization of Highland clans, they shared the Saxon distaste for Norman attempts to impose feudalism. From the 16th century onwards, this ethnically orientated unionist narrative was overlaid with religion as the Reformation placed Scotland and England in the community of Protestant nations. Consequently, when in 1603 James VI of Scotland acceded to the English throne as James I, the seeds of union had already been sown.

The union of the crowns provided the catalyst for further debate about the benefits of union, but the main innovation was to bring political and commercial aspects of the question into consideration along with the religious. During the revolutionary upheavals of the mid-17th century, the Scots even proposed ecclesiastical union of the British people on Presbyterian lines. And the 1689 revolutionary settlement could be seen not merely as the restoration of the ancient constitution but also as the institutionalization of Scots Presbyterian principles.

But the eventual union in 1707 came about in inauspicious circumstances. Having in 1701 turned to the Hanoverians to resolve the royal succession crisis, the English were concerned that the Scots would not follow suit and might restore the Jacobite line, opening up the possibility of intense conflict. Union was one means of avoiding this. At the same time, the Scots were vulnerable. Following the failure of their own imperial enterprise (Darien, or New Caledonia, in the Caribbean), they desperately needed access to trade and empire and this was the carrot the English dangled before them. The outcome, expressed in the 1707 settlement, was the establishment of a common set of legislative, executive, and fiscal—though not judicial—arrangements for the new kingdom of Great Britain.

Some Scots jurists have argued that the Treaty of Union is fundamental law, analogous to a modern constitutional settlement. These arguments have only been made in the post-war period, before which no one seemed to question the fact that this was an incorporating union founded on parliamentary sovereignty. Following the 1707 Treaty, 45 Scottish MPs and 16 representative peers simply joined the Westminster Parliament without even a general election being held, making the point unequivocally that Scotland had been incorporated into an Anglo-centric British state. Guarantees were provided in the Articles of Union to protect the distinctive legal and educational systems and the Presbyterian system of church government. But these statements of political intent had no binding status, and some—such as the requirement that Scottish university professors be practising members of the Church of Scotland—have been overridden by ordinary legislation without contention.

Ireland. Union with Ireland was altogether different. From the 12th century onwards, Ireland had been subject to English attempts at domination. Initially this was through military campaigns, but after the Irish rejected the Reformation the English embarked on a programme of colonization. This involved a policy of land confiscation and plantation by which Irish lands were handed over to English and Scottish Protestant settlers. By the end of the 17th century, the land possessions of Anglo-Protestant settler landlords amounted to 85 per cent of the country. They also acquired complete control of the Irish Parliament, passing a series of penal laws that imposed political and civil disabilities on the great majority of Irish Catholics. By 1690, with the defeat of James II's army—supported by Irish Catholics—at the Battle of the Boyne, the Protestant Ascendancy was complete.

During this period, the Irish Parliament had been preserved, though it remained a dependent legislature. This was formally expressed in Poynings's Law of 1494, which stated that the Irish Parliament could meet only when authorized by the (English) king and which required all legislation to receive prior approval of the English Privy Council. Subordination was further entrenched by the Dependency of Ireland Act of 1720, which declared that the British Parliament maintained 'full power and authority to make laws and statutes of sufficient validity to bind the Kingdom and people of Ireland'. Confirming Ireland's colonial status, it frustrated the aspirations of Irish Protestants to acquire constitutional equality with the English. After the 1798 Rebellion of United Irishmen, which had been influenced by the republican ideals of the American and French revolutions, the British determined that the only lasting foundation for security lay in the union of Ireland with Britain. In 1801, the Irish Parliament was dissolved and incorporated into the Westminster Parliament. In a formal sense, a new state—the United Kingdom of Great Britain and Ireland—was created. The 1801 Act, marking the apotheosis of the principle of parliamentary sovereignty, unified legal authority throughout the islands.

This new state was doomed from the outset. Prime Minister Pitt had quietly conceded Catholic emancipation as part of the Union negotiations. After the Irish Parliament had been dissolved, however, George III vetoed this proposal as contravening his coronation oath to preserve the Protestant religion. The king's action made Pitt's position impossible, and he immediately resigned. The king's manoeuvre also ensured that in the eyes of the great majority of the Irish population the Union lacked legitimacy. From the outset, the Irish lobbied first for Catholic emancipation (achieved in 1829), and then for home rule.

Irish Home Rule, the attempt to reconcile aspirations of Irish nationalism within the frame of the British state, became the dominant political issue of the late 19th century. Home Rule Bills were rejected in 1886 and 1893, causing a fundamental split within the Liberal Party. The third Bill, introduced in 1912, was enacted in the face of Lords' opposition only through the procedures of the Parliament Act 1911. The resulting delay led to its suspension because of the war, which gave time for Ulster Protestants opposed to home rule to raise a private army. This was financed by leading Conservatives and Unionists and justified on the grounds that the Liberal Government had 'seized upon despotic power by fraud' (Bonar Law) and such a despotic use of power 'might justify what was technically conspiracy or rebellion' (Dicey).

As it turned out, the threat of sedition in Ulster was overtaken by events. The failure of the Irish Party, despite majority support in Ireland, to achieve through parliamentary means what it had been seeking since 1885 contributed to frustrations and splits. What followed in quick succession was the Easter Rising in 1916, the electoral success of Sinn Féin, the formation of the Dáil, the Irish War of Independence (1919–21), and then the Anglo-Irish Treaty by which Ireland—with the exception of the six counties of Northern Ireland—seceded from the UK. Consequently, the only part of the Government of Ireland Act 1920 to be implemented was—ironically—home rule within the British state for the six counties of Northern Ireland which maintained a Protestant and Unionist majority.

Empire

Constitutional historians often treat the 18th century as a period of quiescence. After extended 17th-century conflict, the British experienced stability. There may have been abortive Jacobite insurrections in 1715 and 1745, but there were no great revolutions. It was over this period that the conventions of modern parliamentary government evolved. But this is a purely domestic view: a rather different picture emerges from a geo-political perspective. Between 1688 and 1815 the nature of the British state changed dramatically, being transformed from an agrarian to an industrial society and from a relatively weak, insular state into a major European power. During this era, Britain established a standing army and navy, engaged in what has been called the Second Hundred Years War against France, and acquired an extensive empire. The creation of Great Britain in 1707 led in the following century to the formation of what imperialists called 'Greater Britain'.

The basic thesis of Sir John Seeley's influential lectures on *The Expansion of England* (1883) was that the British Empire was fundamentally different from the ancient empires of the Persians, Romans, or Turks. Founded mainly on settlement rather than conquest, 'Greater Britain is a real enlargement of the English State' and it 'carries across the seas not merely the English race but the authority of the English Government'. Wherever English people went, there was England: in New England, New Jersey, and New York, with British people too in New South Wales and Nova Scotia. Unlike other major empires, there was no (Rationalist) imperial project: 'We seem, as it were, to have conquered and peopled half the world in a fit of absence of mind.'

Seeley's point was that in its original incarnation the British Empire was founded on colonial settlement. Its hub was in North America, where the settlers' intention had been to transplant a liberal version of English governmental arrangements. Unlike in Ireland, these colonies did not have native Parliaments, but the dictates of geography meant that in practice they had great autonomy. Tensions in imperial relations emerged, however, once the Revolution of 1688 established the principle of the sovereign authority of the Westminster Parliament. Formally global and absolute, Parliament did not always recognize that this principle must be tempered by practical—perhaps even constitutional—considerations.

The critical issue concerned financing of the military. Having modernized military finance at home by replacing feudal tenure (with its attendant military service) with parliamentary grants raised through taxation, the question arose whether a contribution to these costs should be imposed on the colonies. In levying taxation that was not subject to approval by colonial assemblies, however, Parliament seemed to be depriving the colonists of the same safeguards it had struggled over centuries to maintain at home. When the Westminster Parliament refused to yield, 13 of the 18 American colonies raised armies and in 1776 declared themselves independent. After eight years of war, Britain was obliged to recognize their independence.

The success of the American Revolution irrevocably altered the constitutional arrangements of the British settler empire. The authority of the crown remained the formal principle, but it was now tempered by the clear practical limitations of London's capacity to govern from the metropolis. During the 19th century, the overriding issue for settler colonies was restriction on their powers of self-government, illustrated by the extensive powers given to appointed governors. But from mid-century, powers of responsible government were gradually conferred on the settler colonies, leading to the creation of the Dominions of Canada in 1867, Australia in 1901, New Zealand in 1907, and South Africa in 1910. This constituted an unparalleled devolution of power by an imperial authority. Later, in the Statute of Westminster of 1931, the Westminster Parliament declared that it would no longer legislate for a Dominion without its request and consent, thereby relinquishing its untrammelled authority across the Empire. Settler colonies had, to all intents and purposes, become autonomous states within the British Commonwealth of Nations.

Alongside settler colonies, a 'second British empire' had grown up: this was an empire of conquest rather than settlement. This is not to overlook the fact that the foundation of settler colonies had resulted in the displacement—even genocide—of aboriginal populations, or indeed the extent to which liberal arrangements of settler self-government were underpinned by the institution of slavery. The point is merely that this second empire was explicitly founded on authoritarian rule over subordinate peoples. Driven by commerce, trade, and resource exploitation, this empire spanned the Caribbean, Africa, Asia, and beyond, an empire on which the sun never set.

From the constitutional perspective, Burke had argued that a major expansion of authoritarian power abroad would inevitably unsettle the balance of the constitution at home. His argument had little impact on British imperial ambition, but it did influence the manner of governing. Where imperialists saw a barbaric society needing the blessings of civilization, Burke recognized a morality and culture different from—but equal to—that of the west. This indicated an unresolved tension in the practices of imperial government. Should the British seek modernization through formal legal instruments or work within the grain of local culture and practice? Should the maintenance of 'peace, order and good government' throughout the colonies be advanced through the imposition of modern legal forms or should native laws be retained and respected? In practice, British rule generally sought to accommodate indigenous ways and collaborate with indigenous elites, a practice that became known as 'indirect rule'. This became the governing principle: maximize experience and minimize rationalistic, modernizing governmental schemes.

A similar pragmatism shaped the ways in which territories evolved from crown colonies to self-government. During the First World War—a war which the British Empire entered as a single entity—India mutated into a modified Dominion, leading to dyarchy in the inter-war period (in which elected Indian Ministers assumed responsibility for a range of domestic tasks) and eventually to independence in 1947. That India—and others—were able to form republics yet remain in the Commonwealth owes much to what had been learned from the complications of

Anglo-Irish post-1914 history. The Second World War was the watershed. The self-governing nations of the Empire had entered the war through declarations of their own Parliaments, itself indicative of the loosening of imperial bonds. Immediately after the war the process of self-government and independence for the vast majority of Britain's 52 dependent territories commenced. Britain maintained supervisory responsibility for long enough to be involved in the drafting of independence constitutions. This was a delicate exercise, especially with respect to protections for minorities—ethnic, religious, linguistic—in the new state, and the difficulties entailed in the export of the Westminster system were greatly underestimated. Although the new constitutions were invariably drafted on the parliamentary model, many were subsequently amended and presidential systems established.

The essential point of this potted history is that, throughout a period of dramatic growth in both the scale and complexity of the Empire, its legal form remained fixed. Sovereignty was illimitable and perpetual. And since no limits on the formal authority of the Crown-in-Parliament were conceivable, changing relations between the metropolis and the peripheries had to be effected informally and pragmatically by political and administrative rather than legal methods. One word that remained taboo was federalism, entailing a written constitution, the formal demarcation of jurisdictional responsibility between the centre and the peripheries, and the establishment of a supreme court to police the division. Power may have been exercised federally in practice but, whether with respect to relations between the several nations of the British Isles or between the imperial authority and its dependent colonies, federalism as a formal system was anathema to British constitutional thought.

European Union

The issue of federalism nonetheless loomed large over domestic political debates throughout the post-war period. This was mainly attributable to the UK's involvement in the project of European integration, an uncertain venture which has veered between establishing a common market and realizing a federal United States of Europe. With respect to the former, the British have been equivocal, often sounding sceptical while acquiescing in continuing integration in practice. But with respect to the latter, they have been consistently opposed. Ambivalence about UK involvement in the project eventually culminated in a referendum on continuing membership of the European Union (EU) in 2016 which, following a 52–48 per cent vote for exit, led to formal withdrawal on 31 January 2020.

The UK was not a founder signatory to the Treaty of Rome (1957) which created the European Economic Community (EEC), later the European Community (EC) and most recently the EU. Because of its imperial legacy and close trading ties to British Commonwealth countries, the UK did not then consider its primary economic relations to be with Europe. It was also believed that membership would entail a loss of national sovereignty, something that—being bound up in centuries of constitutional rhetoric—could not be countenanced.

During the 1960s, views about trading relations changed and in 1973 the UK, led by a Conservative government, eventually joined the EEC. Concerns about the implications of membership caused the incoming Labour government in 1975 to hold a referendum on whether the UK should remain in the Community. 67.2 per cent answered in the affirmative, but controversy over the implications for sovereignty continued to permeate debate.

The European Communities Act 1972, which gave effect in domestic law to this 'new legal order', was a masterpiece of concise legislative drafting. Stating that all rights and obligations 'from time to time arising by or under the Treaties . . . are without further enactment to be given legal effect', few grasped its radical implications. It was widely felt that, holding a veto over any proposed new powers, the UK retained control. But as the Union evolved, decision-making was streamlined, with majority voting becoming standard. The claim that Parliament had final say over the adoption of new social or economic regulations therefore became strained.

Furthermore, immersed in the traditions of supreme law-making by Parliament, British politicians seemed oblivious to the fact that the European Court of Justice (ECJ), having quickly established itself as guardian of this new legal order, could itself be a major source of law. Their rulings, especially in devising the principles of the *supremacy of European law* (requiring European law to prevail over any conflict with domestic law), and *direct effect* (conferring rights and obligations to be directly enforced by individuals in the courts of member states), seriously compromised the orthodox doctrine of parliamentary sovereignty.

Operating as the constitutional court of the European legal order, the ECJ gradually constructed a federal legal system that was binding on the legal systems of member states. After years of avoiding the question of its primacy, the point was finally accepted by English courts in the early 1990s. In the *Factortame* litigation, the House of Lords suspended the operation of the Merchant Shipping Act 1988 after the ECJ had ruled that its provisions were contrary to obligations in the Treaty of Rome. 'Whatever limitation of its sovereignty Parliament accepted when it enacted the European Communities Act 1972', the Law Lords held, 'was entirely voluntary.'

This ruling generated fierce debate among British constitutional lawyers. Traditionalists asserted that such a restriction was supposed to be constitutionally impossible while modifiers contended that Parliament could bind itself as to the 'manner and form' of subsequent legislation. Meanwhile modernizers argued that constitutional law could no longer be reduced to the simple rule that whatever Parliament enacts is law: it must now be seen as a system of fundamental constitutional principles. This opened up basic jurisprudential disputes to which we will return in the following chapters.

Following the completion of the single market programme, in 1992 the EU moved to the next, essentially federalist stage of the project which included the launch of a single currency, the euro, in 1999. This was marked by a period of growing scepticism within the UK about the project, signified politically by the rising influence of the United Kingdom Independence Party (UKIP) and constitutionally by pledges from all major political parties not to transfer new powers to the EU without holding a referendum. These developments eventually came to a head in 2015 when the Conservatives were returned as a majority government, having pledged an in/out referendum on EU membership. Held in June 2016, it resulted in a majority voting to leave.

What followed constitutes one of the most dramatic periods in modern British constitutional history. Having advocated remain, David Cameron felt obliged to resign as PM, to be replaced by Theresa May. After negotiating a withdrawal agreement with the EU which was voted down three times in Parliament, in 2019 May also resigned. When she was replaced by Boris Johnson, there followed an even more tumultuous period during which many conventions of parliamentary government simply broke down. Johnson inherited a minority government that could not go to the polls because the power to dissolve Parliament had effectively been transferred to the Commons in the Fixed-term Parliaments Act 2011. He therefore prorogued Parliament for a five-week period, only to find the Supreme Court declaring the action 'unlawful, null, and of no effect'. The government then became subservient to a Parliament that, in an unprecedented move, took control of the Commons Order Paper and passed a Bill mandating the PM to request an extension to the EU exit date.

This turbulent period came to an abrupt end in December 2019 when minority parties eventually agreed to the holding of a general election. An Act was passed circumventing the need to obtain a two-thirds majority under the provisions of the 2011 Act and in the election the Conservatives were returned with a large overall majority of 80. The UK formally left the EU at the end of January 2020, apparently bringing this chaotic phase to a close.

But things were not so simple. Having exited the EU on the mantra of 'taking back control', it might have been assumed that the supremacy of Parliament in relation to EU law would be unequivocally restored. Legislation required to effect this was the EU (Withdrawal) Act 2018, which repealed the European Communities Act but provided that 'retained EU law' would continue to have domestic effect. This, together with the EU (Withdrawal Agreement) Act 2020 and the EU (Future Relationship) Act 2020, incorporating the terms of withdrawal in domestic law, not only indicated the continuing impact of EU law within the UK but also demonstrated the extent to which government by decree would prevail over parliamentary control.

Devolution

EU membership demonstrated how national sovereignty can be circumscribed by the status of 'member state' within a federal relationship. But sovereignty has also been questioned by the rekindling of national identities within the UK. Over the past half century, the status of the northern six counties of Ireland, left unresolved in the 1920s, and demands for devolution in Scotland and Wales have all become constitutional preoccupations. Initially, membership of the EU meant these issues could be managed administratively and their constitutional significance repressed. But the UK's exit from the EU has brought to the fore the constitutional dimensions to home rule movements.

The Labour government elected in 1997 placed the devolution of power to the non-English parts of the United Kingdom at the core of its programme. With respect to Scotland and Wales, this policy was a legacy of eighteen years of Conservative rule in which radical changes like de-industrialization, privatization, de-regulation, and restructuring the welfare state lacked support in the Celtic regions and left the government with scarcely enough of those MPs to run the Scottish and Welsh Offices. The legitimacy deficit was most strongly felt in Scotland where a Claim of Right was drafted in 1989, asserting the 'sovereign right of the Scottish people to determine the form of Government best suited to their needs'. Endorsed by 58 of Scotland's 72 MPs, 7 of their 8 Members of the European Parliament, 59 of the 65 local councils, and numerous churches, trade unions, and civil bodies, the Claim led to the establishment of an (unofficial) Scottish Constitutional Convention which drew up a scheme for home rule. This provided the template for the Labour government's proposals.

The government's devolution programme was implemented in the Scotland Act 1998, a scheme of devolved legislative powers to a Scottish Parliament in Edinburgh, and the Government of Wales Act 1998, a scheme of devolved executive powers to a National Assembly for Wales in Cardiff (though subsequently extended). The 1998 Acts had been preceded by referendums in Scotland and Wales. Although the Scottish referendum yielded a resoundingly positive result (75:25), the Welsh voted in favour of an Assembly by the narrowest of margins (50.3:49.7).

During the same year, the Northern Ireland Act was passed. This established a Northern Ireland Assembly with devolved legislative powers. But the situation here, as ever, was fundamentally different. After the post-First World War upheavals in Ireland, in 1922 a Parliament with devolved powers of home rule had been established for Northern Ireland. This Parliament replicated Westminster practices and, in the tense conditions in which a sizeable minority rejected the legitimacy of the arrangement, the Protestant majority ran the province to the benefit of their own community. When the grievances of the Catholic minority were turned into civil rights campaigns during the late 1960s, tension was strained to breaking point. After violence erupted, the British government and army became increasingly involved in the domestic affairs of the province, and in 1972 the Stormont Parliament was suspended and later abolished. The 1998 Act thus marked the end of a period of direct rule from London. The settlement it introduced was much more than a scheme of legislative devolution: deploying Rationalist principles of institutional design, it signalled nothing less than a systematic attempt to bring about social change through a novel constitution-building exercise.

The backdrop to these reforms was the Belfast (or Good Friday) Agreement signed by the UK and Irish governments in 1998. Marking the outcome of a peace process and ratified by referendums in both Ireland and the North, it initiated a constitutional process designed to encourage nationalists and unionists to work together to govern the province. The establishment of an Executive containing both communities and governing as a dyarchy forms one of three strands of the Agreement; the others provide for a North–South Ministerial Council for discussion and implementation of limited shared executive functions, and a British–Irish Intergovernmental Conference to develop longer-term strategy.

The Agreement sought to bolster the legitimacy of constitutional arrangements within the province through such initiatives as decommissioning of paramilitary weapons, prisoner release schemes, the reconstitution of the police and prosecution services, the regulation of symbols and parades, and the strengthening of equality laws. Recognizing that the adoption of Westminster practices exacerbated political tensions, these have been replaced by innovative constitutional mechanisms. And each side has accepted that the people of Northern Ireland have the right to self-determination, including the right to secede should this be the wish of a future majority.

These various schemes have created a mosaic, with the governing arrangements for each part of the UK now significantly varying. The devolution schemes all contain modernizing elements, evident in voting systems, assembly procedures, and executive decision-making arrangements. But reforms that strengthen legitimacy in the regions raise new issues of legitimacy at the centre, not least because the Westminster Parliament no longer regularly legislates for the whole of the UK. As was graphically illustrated by the different National Health Service responses to the 2020–2 Coronavirus pandemic, the UK government no longer carries UK-wide responsibility for public service delivery. Lip service continues to be paid to the continuing sovereign authority of the Westminster Parliament, but recent developments have strained this almost to breaking point.

The catalyst was the 2011 Holyrood election in which the Scottish National Party (SNP) was returned with an overall majority on a manifesto pledge of holding a referendum on Scottish independence. Although this was beyond the powers of the Scottish Parliament under the devolution scheme, it was conceded by the UK government. Held in 2014, on a turnout of around 85 per cent, the referendum yielded a majority vote against independence (55.3 per cent to 44.7 per cent). Concerned about the result, however, the three main UK parties had pledged in advance of the result to extend the powers of the Scottish Parliament. These additional powers, especially relating to finance, were conferred by the Scotland Act 2016.

The 2016 Act also made some constitutional innovations. It stated that 'the Scottish Parliament and the Scottish Government are a permanent part of the United Kingdom's constitutional arrangements' and 'are not to be abolished except on the basis of a decision of the people of Scotland voting in a referendum'. It also put onto statutory foundation the Sewel convention that Westminster 'will not normally legislate with regard to devolved matters without the consent of the Scottish Parliament'. In 2017, similar constitutional protections were included in the Wales Act. These developments signal the beginning of the end of Dicey's doctrine of parliamentary sovereignty, and the incremental evolution of an asymmetric federal scheme for the UK.

The tensions implicit in this evolving scheme have been further heightened by Brexit. Although the 2016 referendum yielded a majority for leaving, Northern Ireland and Scotland recorded majorities (56–44 per cent and 62–38 per cent respectively) in favour of remaining in the EU. This divergence strained relations throughout the negotiating process, including claims that withdrawal without the consent of these devolved legislatures was illegitimate. It has also had serious post-exit consequences.

The SNP argued that Scotland had been removed from the EU against its will. When in 2021 they received a further mandate to govern, they pledged to hold a second independence referendum, intended for 2023 though, following upheavals in the SNP, now indefinitely postponed. But post-Brexit Scottish independence, it should be emphasized, has much wider ramifications. In 2016, for example, the SNP intended to maintain sterling as its currency, to have monetary policy overseen by the Bank of England, and as fellow EU member states there would obviously be no trade barriers. The issue of trade barriers has remained highly contentious in Northern Ireland, the one area of the UK that maintains a land border with an EU member state. The erection of customs barriers here was felt to threaten the peace process and accords established in the Good Friday Agreement. Consequently, a Protocol to the Withdrawal Agreement was negotiated under which EU customs union arrangements still apply in Northern Ireland, with the customs

3. 'We used to call it United'.

border established in the Irish Sea. The working arrangements for this have generated disputes between the UK and EU, and are such a source of discontent among unionist groups in Northern Ireland that from May 2022 to 2023 they have blocked appointment of a Northern Ireland Executive.

State, nation, and citizen

State, nation, and citizen are three modern concepts that do not easily fit the British experience. In the modern narrative, the people of a defined territory conceive themselves as forming a unity (a nation) and establish an association (a state) of which they become equal members (citizens). The terms of this association are then expressed in a basic pact, the written constitution that takes effect as fundamental law. The reality is that states are constructed from above, but in this singular moment of imaginative constitutional self-reflection, the people conceive themselves to be authors of their own governing terms.

Each of these modern elements confounds understanding of the British experience. The British have never embraced the idea of the state as an expression of the institutional form of the association. The closest legal symbol is the crown, which signifies the monarch in his public capacity. It is in this sense that reference is made to His Majesty's government, or to crown servants, or the Royal Courts of Justice. But the jurisprudence surrounding the concept of the crown remains blurred, and no simple distinction can be made between monarch and crown, person and office, private and public.

This obfuscation permeates the laws of nationality and citizenship. English law is tied to ancient bonds of allegiance by which subjects owed fealty to their king. This has its roots in *Calvin's Case* (1608) in which it was held that those born in Scotland after the accession of James VI (of Scotland) to the throne of England (as James I) were naturalized in England and entitled to the full protection of its law. Recognition of allegiance as a personal bond meant that all the peoples of the Empire became subjects of the king. But this lack of a modern law of citizenship presented problems once Britain experienced various waves of Commonwealth immigration from the mid-20th century onwards.

It led to the modern law of British citizenship, constructed by the Immigration Act 1971 and the British Nationality Act 1981, being shaped by the exigencies of immigration control. This created a complicated set of citizenship categories—British Citizen, British Dependent Territories Citizen, British Overseas Citizen, British Subject, and British Protected Person—with only the first category carrying the right of abode, leading to continuing criticism about its racially discriminatory impact.

Fixed within a monarchical conception of authority, the law of the constitution has not been systematically adapted to modern notions of the state, nation, or citizen. In this chapter, I have recounted how the English state (which covered England and Wales) during the 18th century was transformed into a British state founded on Protestantism and set to work to build an empire. As one of its first colonial projects, Ireland has never been fully integrated, and in that sense there has never really been a UK state. This is evidenced today by the peculiar status of Northern Ireland, which the British state is pledged to relinquish once a majority of the population of the province signals that preference, which, given the upheavals of Brexit, is coming ever closer. But now that Britain's imperial mission is over and the religious basis of its political identity is anachronistic, the ties that bind the English and Scots are rapidly unravelling. In 1886, Dicey wrote that 'there exists in Europe no country so completely at unity with itself as Great Britain'. How things have changed. Whether the British state continues to have a rationale is today very much in question.

Chapter 6
Civil liberty

During the modern era the British constitution has attracted high praise for the value it places on liberty. This theme featured prominently in the work of Whig constitutional historians for whom liberties were never simply the product of monarchical concession but were, in Blackstone's words, 'coeval with our form of government'. Liberties might occasionally have been suppressed by overbearing kings, but 'the vigour of our free constitution has always delivered the nation from these embarrassments' and has always managed to resettle 'the balance of our rights and liberties...to its proper level'. The great landmark documents—Magna Carta (1215), the Petition of Right (1628), the Bill of Rights (1689)—conferred no new rights. They merely restated their existence as, in the words of the Bill of Rights, 'the true, ancient and indubitable rights of the people of this kingdom'. It is this tradition that led Montesquieu to claim in 1748 that Britain was the 'one nation in the world whose constitution had political liberty for its direct purpose'.

In the light of this claimed inheritance, this chapter has three main objectives. It first examines the nature of these liberties and the arrangements by which they are protected. In this respect, it sketches the manner in which (understood cumulatively) 'civil liberty' has been maintained. Secondly, it considers how the extended powers of modern government have eroded these traditional safeguards. Finally, it assesses the significance of recent judicial and legislative attempts to restore the protection of liberty in response to the growing powers of government. The question the reader might bear in mind is whether Montesquieu's claim still pertains. Does the contemporary constitution have 'political liberty for its direct purpose'?

The constitution of liberty

Blackstone organized the basic liberties protected by the constitution into three main categories. First, there is the right of *personal security*, which protects the life, bodily integrity, health, and reputation of the person. From this basic right evolve the rules of criminal law, poor law provision for the necessities of life, and the law of defamation. Second is the right to *personal liberty*, guaranteeing freedom from imprisonment without due cause and lawful trial, and freedom of movement within and beyond the realm. The final category is the right of *private property*, which includes the free use, enjoyment, and disposition of property regulated only by the law of the land, including taxation by parliamentary authorization.

These rights, Blackstone noted, were safeguarded by certain institutional 'pillars of liberty'. The most important is Parliament, which imposes limitations on the king's prerogatives, seeks the redress of grievances before acquiescing in taxation, and maintains a right of access to the courts for remedying wrongs. Other institutional arrangements are also important, two in particular. The first is trial by jury, i.e. judgement by one's peers. This provision, rooted in ancient Saxon practice, is claimed to stem from ch. 39 of Magna Carta: 'No freeman shall be taken or imprisoned... except by the legal judgment of his peers or by the law of the land.' The second arrangement, which also derives from ch. 39, is the writ of habeas corpus by which the court requires that legal cause for detention be shown. During the Victorian era, these auxiliary protections—overseen by a judiciary whose

Civil liberty

independence had been signalled by s. 3 of the Act of Settlement of 1701—were transformed by Dicey into a formal constitutional principle. He called this principle the 'rule of law'.

For Dicey, the rule of law has three meanings. First, no one can be punished except for a 'distinct breach of the law established in the ordinary legal manner before the ordinary Courts of the land'. Dicey here highlights the tradition of strict legality running through the British system of government. Secondly, the rule of law embodies the principle of equality before the law: 'the universal subjection of all classes to one law administered by the ordinary Courts.' Disputes are to be adjudicated in accordance with a common set of rules, applied to ordinary subjects and Ministers of the Crown alike. The third sense of the rule of law is more elaborate. It embodies the conviction that the constitution itself comes from the ordinary law of the land. The 'law of the constitution', Dicey states, is 'not the source but the consequence of the rights of individuals'. Civil liberty is ensured not by the formal declaration of rights but as a result of constant struggle and vigilance leading to outcomes recorded and protected in judicial decisions.

This safeguarding of liberty through the workings of the 'rule of law' contrasts sharply with the modern practice of formal declarations of rights. Here, rights to personal liberty are *deduced* from the constitution, whereas in the English tradition 'constitutional principles' are *induced* from various court rulings on personal rights. For Dicey, the English approach is preferable. Being the work of many 'whose labours gradually framed the complicated set of laws and institutions which we call the Constitution', it may form a less than tidy arrangement. The Habeas Corpus Acts 'declare no principle and define no rights', but they are 'for practical purposes worth a hundred constitutional articles guaranteeing individual liberty'.

The reason for this claimed superiority arises from institutional arrangements. When the source of personal liberty is located in written constitutions, those rights can be suspended or repealed. But where the 'right to individual freedom is part of the constitution because it is part of the ordinary law of the land', Dicey contended that 'the right is one which can hardly be destroyed without a thorough revolution in the institutions and manners of the nation'. As the product of long struggle institutionalized in the practices of governing, Dicey maintained that 'the securities for personal freedom are in England as complete as the laws can make them'.

Rule by law

The principle of the rule of law appears to be opposed to the fundamental doctrine of parliamentary sovereignty. Since Parliament has absolute authority in law-making, how can legislation inimical to liberty be prevented? Dicey recognized the problem but claimed that in two important ways parliamentary sovereignty actually supports the rule of law. The first is that the commands of Parliament must be approved by its constituent parts, i.e. the Commons, the Lords, and the Royal Assent. This promotes deliberation and ensures that Parliament will look 'with disfavour and jealousy on all exemptions of officials from the ordinary liabilities of citizens or from the jurisdiction of the ordinary courts'. The second way is that legislation is strictly construed by judges, a tradition of legal formality that 'constantly hampers (and sometimes with great injury to the public) the action of the executive'. The courts 'will prevent, at any rate where personal liberty is concerned, the exercise by the government of any sort of discretionary power'. Parliament will confer broad powers only when absolutely necessary and a judiciary infused with the common law 'spirit of legality' will remain vigilant in interpreting restrictions on personal liberty.

In this constitutional tradition, law is a species of command. Since law imposes constraints, the less we have of it, the greater will be our freedom. This is the core of the British tradition of civil liberty: we appeal to our ancient liberties to protect us from the rigours of the law. The price of liberty is eternal vigilance: civil liberty is preserved by maintaining a vibrant political and parliamentary discourse. This is why freedom of the press is so highly prized. It is also why Parliament maintains extensive privileges with respect to freedom of speech, freedom from arrest, the ability to regulate its own proceedings, and the right to punish for breach of these privileges or for contempt of Parliament. And this elucidates the point of Montesquieu's claim that the 'state will perish when legislative power is more corrupt than executive power'.

Parliament's role is pivotal, but it must be assisted by a judiciary that applies the law in a manner that is both strict and favourable to liberty. The judiciary's historic role is illustrated by the landmark case of *Entick v Carrington* (1765) in which judges rejected the argument that a Minister's warrant was sufficient to authorize the search of premises and the seizure of papers alleged to contain evidence of seditious intent. Rebuffing the government's argument that this action was vital for reasons of state, the court claimed that 'the common law does not understand that kind of reasoning'. The judiciary explicitly rejected the claim that official status was sufficient of itself to confer lawful authority. 'If it is law', the judges declared, 'it will be found in our books. If it is not found there, it is not law.'

Crucial to Dicey's conception of the rule of law is the partnership between Parliament and judiciary. This partnership discloses a peculiarly British version of the separation of powers, a notion most clearly expressed by Lord Diplock in *Duport Steels v Sirs* (1980): 'It cannot be too strongly emphasized that the British constitution, though largely unwritten, is firmly based on the separation of powers: Parliament makes the laws, the judiciary interprets them.'

Dicey illustrated this partnership with reference to the way the Habeas Corpus Act of 1679 put the common law writ on a statutory foundation. But this example also highlighted a potential weakness. Although the writ of habeas corpus—in denying the crown any inherent power of detention—had performed an important role in the 17th-century struggles, its continuing usefulness came to depend on parliamentary restraint. The difficulty has been that once parliamentary supremacy over the crown was confirmed by the 1688 Revolution, Parliament became more sanguine about conferring executive powers by statute. In one of its very first post-Revolution Acts (1 W&M c. 2), for example, the king was granted power to 'apprehend and detain such persons as He shall find just cause to suspect are conspiring against the Government'. In the following century, similar statutory powers drastically curtailed the effectiveness of habeas corpus to protect even those who sought reform of the constitution rather than the revolutionary overthrow of the government.

This problem was experienced with dramatic effect in 19th-century Ireland where a series of Acts granting wide powers of arrest and detention were passed. Burke had prophesied that authoritarian rule abroad might eventually corrupt liberal practices at home and this 19th-century Irish practice did indeed provide a model for the drafting of wartime emergency legislation during the 20th century. Legislation such as the Official Secrets Act 1911, the Defence of the Realm Acts 1914–15, and the Emergency Powers Act 1920 contained extensive powers of search, seizure, and detention alongside restrictions on freedom of speech, expression, and movement. The principle of the 'rule of law' extolled by Dicey had come to mean 'rule by such law as Parliament enacts'. Modern legislation, now incorporated in such statutes as the Civil Contingencies Act 2004, the terrorism legislation of 2000–1, and the Public Order Act 2023, has considerably undermined Dicey's confident belief that Parliament will be slow to approve provisions that confer broad discretionary powers.

But what of judicial protection? The record of the judiciary during much of the 20th century with respect to personal liberty has been mixed. The tone was set early on in cases such as *R. v Halliday, ex parte Zadig* (1917), where the judiciary departed from a strict construction to reject habeas corpus challenges to the legality of detaining persons of 'hostile origin or associations'. Likewise, the judicial role with respect to social and industrial conflicts and restrictions on radical political movements has been particularly weak. This is exemplified by the case of *Duncan v Jones* (1936), which upheld the power of the police to criminalize assemblies by breaking up meetings that might lead to a breach of the peace. By the 1980s, cases of miscarriage of justice such as the Birmingham Six, the Guildford Four, the Maguire Seven, and the Bridgewater Four were casting serious doubts on judges' impartiality. So when the judiciary sought to maintain a ban on the reporting of the memoirs of a former MI5 officer in the *Spycatcher* saga, their claim to be acting as guardians of a 'constitution of liberty' seemed scarcely credible (see Figure 3).

From a constitutional perspective, however, the case that best illustrates the limitations of the common-law method of protecting liberty is that of *Malone v Metropolitan Police Commissioner* (1979). In an action that paralleled *Entick*'s case, Malone brought an action against the police for tapping his telephone, the authorization for which had been granted by the Home Secretary purely by administrative action, i.e. without explicit legal authority. But Malone's action failed on the ground that interception took place on telephone lines outside his property. Since there had been no interference with Malone's property or other rights, it was not deemed unlawful. In the words of the judge: 'England is not a country where everything is forbidden except what is expressly permitted: it is a country where everything is permitted except what is expressly forbidden.' Such a broad permission is one that the police and security services are particularly well placed to exploit. Whatever else it stands for, *Malone* demonstrates that the tradition of protecting liberties by way of 'ordinary law' had distinct limitations.

BOOKS AND ARTS

My country, Wright or wrong

SPYCATCHER. By Peter Wright. Viking. 392 pages. $19.95

> The Economist has
> 1.5m readers in 170
> countries. In all but one
> country, our readers
> have on this page a
> review of "Spycatcher",
> a book by an ex-MI5
> man, Peter Wright. The
> exception is Britain,
> where the book, and
> comment on it, have
> been banned. For our
> 420,000 readers there,
> this page is blank—and
> the law is an ass.

Civil liberty

4. *The Economist's* review of *Spycatcher*, 25 July 1987.

Liberty and the growth of administrative government

The personal liberty that Blackstone and Dicey held dear was that enshrined in classical liberalism. Sometimes called negative liberty it expresses a 'freedom from' control by another. It is also a type of liberty that in 18th- and 19th-century Britain was enjoyed only by a very limited class of persons, i.e. male property-holders who had already acquired the right not to be taxed or governed without their consent. From the late 19th century, classical liberalism was challenged by a more radical liberal philosophy that sought equal liberty for all.

This new liberalism contained two main elements. First, it promoted universal political rights, that is, the right of every individual to play an equal role in sending representatives to Parliament. Classical liberals were not necessarily opposed to this aim, but they remained fearful of what they called 'the tyranny of the majority', tending to embrace only a democracy that could be reconciled with what Dicey called our 'inherited traditions of aristocratic government'. The second was the achievement of conditions conducive to equal liberty for all. This objective was more challenging. It required action by government to improve education, health, and social security, providing a platform of basic social and economic entitlements that could help citizens realize their full potential. This objective could hardly be achieved without passing legislation conferring discretionary powers on government agencies, action that was vehemently opposed by classical liberals. The promotion of equality by governmental action, they argued, of necessity undermined liberty and the rule of law.

When 20th-century Liberal and Labour governments sought to promote these positive objectives by legislative means, many raised concerns on constitutional grounds. This became one of the major constitutional controversies of the first half of the 20th century. For many, the judiciary's vigilance in quashing the innovative and sometimes radical policies of Labour-controlled local authorities merely highlighted the common law's inability to adapt to the modern democratic world. When in 1929 Lord Hewart, the Lord Chief Justice and head of the common-law courts, published a book complaining that the acquisition of discretionary powers by the executive was undermining the principles of the constitution, the controversy reached fever-pitch. Never let it be said, he declaimed, 'that liberty and justice, having been won, were suffered to be abstracted, or impaired in a fit of absence of mind'.

Hewart's claim that the growth of governmental powers posed the threat of a 'new despotism' to rival that of the Stuarts in the 17th century may have been constitutional, but it was also intensely political. After all, when as Solicitor-General he represented the government in *Zadig*'s case, he had not seemed unduly troubled by wartime incursions on 'personal liberty'. Similarly, his later ruling in *Duncan v Jones* (1936) in favour of broader police powers to restrict freedom of expression showed little concern about the breadth of discretionary powers he was then recognizing. Such apparently selective intervention led Harold Laski to conclude that, in the guise of providing constitutional oversight, the judiciary had become 'the unconscious servant of a single class in the community'. The inter-war record left a specific constitutional legacy: that of profound distrust in the judiciary's ability to act as (self-appointed) guardians of the constitution.

After the Second World War, the judiciary managed to focus constitutional issues entirely on the challenge posed by the growth of administrative power. 'Our procedure for securing our personal freedom is efficient', asserted Lord Denning in his influential lectures on *Freedom under Law* (1947), but 'our procedure for preventing the abuse of power is not'. The judiciary set themselves the task of developing new procedures and principles for supervising the exercise of public powers conferred by the legislative action of Parliament.

Judicial progress in modernizing these principles and procedures of judicial review was slow and faltering. Even the breakthrough cases of the 1960s—on issues like review for errors of law, procedural unfairness, and prerogative powers—were followed very hesitantly during the following decade. This was perhaps not surprising, because such changes directly cut across central aspects of common-law practice. It was not until the 1980s that Lord Diplock, after almost twenty years on the bench, felt able to state that he regarded the progress made towards creating a system of administrative law as 'the greatest achievement of the English courts in my judicial lifetime'.

What Diplock meant by the creation of a 'system' was that the courts had brought the administrative powers of government under the overarching supervision of the common-law courts. To achieve this, the judiciary made two radical changes. First, the traditional categories of judicial review (natural justice, jurisdiction, manifest unreasonableness) were replaced with more rationalist tests (fairness, legality, irrationality). Secondly, the judiciary recognized that traditional adherence to the ordinary law must be jettisoned in favour of a conceptual distinction between public law and private law.

Once these procedural and conceptual reforms had been introduced, the judges felt emboldened to involve themselves directly in constitutional modernization. They saw their essential task as bolstering the rule of law within a modern constitutional framework. Traditionally, the rule of law expressed a rule of political prudence sheltering within the framework of parliamentary sovereignty. The judicial challenge was to convert the rule of law from political aspiration into juridical principle. After taking the first steps by reformulating the heads of judicial review, they asserted that, rather than being a secondary feature of the constitution, the rule of law has become its fundamental principle.

A significant step exemplifying this claim was taken by Lord Bridge in *X. v Morgan-Grampian* (1991). This case involved a journalist's refusal to reveal who had supplied him with a confidential business plan and was therefore not a case dealing centrally with relationships between government institutions. Holding that the maintenance of the rule of law is just as important to contemporary society as the democratic franchise, Bridge asserted that the rule of law 'rests upon twin foundations: the sovereignty of the Queen in Parliament in making the law and the sovereignty of the Queen's courts in interpreting and applying the law'. This seems at first to be no more than a reformulation of Diplock's classic account of separation of powers. But Bridge's use of the expression 'sovereignty' confounded accepted understanding. In a conventional sense, his statement is nonsensical. Sovereignty is an absolute concept: to divide it is to destroy it. But perhaps this was the objective: presenting traditional formulations in novel ways aids innovative re-conceptualization. In relativizing the respective claims of Parliament and judiciary to make and interpret law, Bridge was pressing home the point that the overarching principle of the British constitution is not sovereignty but legality.

The judiciary has only felt able to make this point explicitly in the new millennium. In *R. v Home Secretary, ex parte Simms* (2000), for example, Lord Hoffmann noted that although the courts acknowledge the sovereignty of Parliament, they nonetheless 'apply principles of constitutionality little different from those which exist in countries where the power of the legislature is expressly limited by a constitutional document'. And in *Jackson v Attorney-General* (2005), Lord Hope confidently took the next step by advancing the bold claim that 'the rule of law enforced by the courts is the ultimate controlling factor on which our constitution is based'. He left amplification of this to Lord Steyn. 'The classic account given by Dicey of the doctrine of the supremacy of Parliament', Steyn asserted in *Jackson*, 'can now be seen to be out of place in the modern United Kingdom.' Parliamentary supremacy (the word he used in preference to sovereignty) might still be the general principle. But since it was created by the judges, 'it is not unthinkable that circumstances could arise where the courts may have to qualify a principle established on a different hypothesis of constitutionalism'.

The claim that the judges *created* the principle, a key tenet of what has become known as 'common-law constitutionalism', is controversial. In modern times, judges have certainly come to *recognize* the doctrine of parliamentary sovereignty; since it is the consequence of 300 years of intense political struggle leading to basic shifts in the sources of governmental authority, they could hardly do otherwise. But Steyn's assertion that the doctrine was created by the judiciary is revolutionary. Contrary to the views of those such as Dicey and Jennings who acknowledged the distinction between constitution and law and therefore the conventional nature of the category 'constitutional law' (discussed above in Chapter 3), Steyn and his fellow legal rationalists promote law over practice, a normative version of constitutional ordering over institutional description, and 'legal constitutionalism' over the inherited practices of the 'political constitution'.

From civil liberties to human rights

The telephone-tapping case of *Malone* is the pivot on which to assess the significance of these judicial developments. The case highlights the limitations of the traditional common-law approach to civil liberties, and in particular the consequences of a failure to draw a distinction between public law and private law. In the constitutional architecture of continental Europe, erected on the distinction between public law and private law, Ministers and their agents are not free to do whatever they want unless there are specific legal restraints. That principle might be correct as a matter of private law in which ordinary persons can do anything the law does not prohibit. But in public law the true principle is that official persons can only act where the law permits. Private persons may be holders of rights, but official persons are impressed with duties.

This distinction acquires a special significance in Malone's case because, having failed in the English courts, Malone took his grievance to the European Court of Human Rights (ECtHR). In 1951, the UK had ratified the European Convention on Human Rights (ECHR), an international treaty that established a charter of civil and political rights which contracting states have pledged to respect. The treaty provides for dispute resolution primarily through the ECtHR, and since 1966 the UK government has accepted the right of individuals to petition the Court. In Malone's case, the Court ruled that the government's action was in breach of its duty under Article 8 of the Convention to maintain respect for the individual's private life and correspondence. Being in breach of its international obligations, the government promptly introduced legislation that established a procedure for authorizing telephone tapping. This was contained in the Interception of Communications Act 1985 (now in the Regulation of Investigatory Powers Act 2000).

Malone's case was hardly unique: since 1966 there have been scores of ECtHR rulings that have found breaches by the UK. Many have led to landmark changes in the law, ranging from the extension of prisoners' rights to the abolition of corporal punishment in schools. But because Britain maintains a distinction between domestic law and international law, the civil rights expressed in the Convention were initially not directly enforceable in British law. Individuals were therefore obliged to exhaust their domestic remedies before petitioning the ECtHR. Similarly, the rulings of the Court could not be directly enforced; they were dependent on governmental action to bring about a change in the law.

This growing influence of European human rights law should be read alongside the domestic movement to rationalize the principles of judicial review and apply them more actively to the supervision of governmental action. The domestic movement has led to the judiciary adopting more rights-protective methods. Rather than taking the traditional approach of focusing on the authority of the public body to act, judges now ask whether and to what extent there has been an interference with an individual right. This puts the onus on the public body to justify its action. Nevertheless, within a constitutional framework that regards judges as the precision instruments of parliamentary intention, there were still distinct limits to the pursuit of activism. It was for this reason that during the 1990s many leading judges publicly advocated the necessity of making the ECHR directly enforceable in domestic courts.

That objective was realized when the Labour government introduced the Human Rights Act 1998 (HRA). This Act, which came into full effect in October 2000, makes provision for the enforcement in domestic law of the rights guaranteed by the Convention.

The 1998 Act makes it 'unlawful for a public authority to act in a way which is incompatible with a Convention right' (s. 6). Additionally, section 3 requires all legislation to be interpreted 'in a way which is compatible with the Convention rights'. This imposes a powerful interpretative obligation on the judiciary, one that runs contrary to discerning its 'plain meaning', the approach traditionally adopted. But the Act recognizes that if legislation cannot be interpreted in such a manner as to render it compatible with Convention rights, the courts are not empowered to strike it down. They can only issue a declaration of incompatibility under section 4, which has no direct legal effect. The legislative provision remains in force, although the government is then authorized to use a fast-track procedure for introducing legislation to achieve compatibility. In this way, the 1998 Act upholds the formal principle of parliamentary sovereignty, though we might note that in 2021 the Supreme Court stated that even this provision had 'qualified' Parliament's sovereignty.

A high-profile illustration of the way this declaratory power operates is *A. v Secretary of State for the Home Department* (2004). The question was whether the courts could review the government's decision to derogate from Article 5 of the ECHR, the right to liberty, in order to establish in Part IV of the Anti-Terrorism, Crime and Security Act 2001 a regime for the indefinite detention of foreign nationals suspected of being international terrorists and who—for legal or practical reasons—could not be deported. Asserting jurisdiction, the House of Lords declared such a regime incompatible with Article 5. The government accepted this ruling, repealed the offending provisions of the 2001 Act, and in 2005 introduced a new Prevention of Terrorism Act. This contained a more graduated system of detention called control orders, a scheme further amended in the Terrorism Prevention and Investigation Measures Act 2011.

This case highlights how the HRA can exacerbate institutional tensions. Granting the executive extensive counter-terrorist powers after 11 September 2001 has led to a series of challenges under the Act which, rather than promoting a partnership between Parliament and judiciary, have made the question of the relative importance of security and liberty a matter of institutional struggle. These are some of the most difficult issues to balance in rights-based regimes and have shaped debate from the moment of the HRA's adoption.

The HRA established a new regime of civil rights protection. These rights range from the right to life, liberty, security, and fair trial to protections over freedom of thought, expression, and assembly. The Act signals a shift away from constitutional protection of civil liberty through parliamentary restraint and strict judicial construction towards a framework in which the judiciary has a leading role as the guardians of enumerated rights. It has not been uncontroversial but, on the whole, the judiciary has managed to avoid the political bear-traps these fresh responsibilities inevitably set up. This is due to their use of a more rationalist, proportionality-based review test. Since the court is evidently a public authority for the purpose of the Act, they must now develop the common law in conformity with those rights. This has led them to develop the idea of common-law constitutional rights, marking a further significant step along the road to rationalization as well as presaging further changes in constitutional ordering. For beyond the practical and political challenges of rights protection lie fundamental conceptual ambiguities arising from the need to reconcile a newly enhanced principle of legality with the tradition of parliamentary sovereignty. But one thing seems certain: contrary to Dicey's contention, the law of the constitution is now the source rather than the consequence of our rights.

These innovations have proved especially controversial in conservative circles. Having pledged to repeal the HRA and replace it with a British Bill of Rights, the Conservative government in 2021 established an Independent Review of the Act, whose terms of reference did not include its repeal. Controversially, however, the publication of that report in December 2021 was accompanied by a government consultation paper proposing to replace the HRA in its entirety with a new British Bill of Rights. This Bill was due to be debated by the Commons in September 2022, but with the replacement of Johnson as PM by Liz Truss, the Bill was withdrawn. The Conservatives evidently are seeking to adjust the relationship between UK courts, the ECtHR, and Parliament, not least by bolstering the principle of parliamentary sovereignty. As things stand presently, however, they remain unclear how best to further that objective.

Chapter 7
Whither the constitution?

Constitutional development

All states are constructed from above, and Britain is no exception. The story begins with the brute fact of a kingly power imposing its rule over a people. But such a power can only sustain itself with the acceptance of those subject to this rule. How is this original usurpation made legitimate? In his classic analysis, Max Weber identified three main sources of legitimacy: *charismatic*, which requires devotion to the exemplary, even sacred, character of a leader; *traditional*, involving acceptance of the authority of immemorial custom; and the *rational*, entailing belief in the rightful nature of a ruler's authority to make law. In the history of governmental forms, these sources of legitimacy follow a sequential arrangement, from ancient to modern. They also suggest an ascending order of clarity, from opaque to transparent.

In the story of British government, we see how monarchical authority is acquired through four critical stages. The first stage distinguishes between the private and public aspects of kingship, between feudal overlordship and official rulership. In the second stage, the representative nature of the office of the crown is recognized as an office held in trust for the public good. The third stage acknowledges the crown's composite character. By incorporating the roles of law-making, law-enforcing, and law-interpreting, this third stage accepts the need for differentiating governmental functions between the king's council, the king's court, and the king-in-Parliament. From this perspective, the constitution provides the means through which rulers and subjects express their beliefs about the authority of government. The British constitution evolves from ancient to modern, from rudimentary to complex. It also evolves from the charismatic, through the traditional, to the rational, though, as Bagehot's account illustrated, during the modern period it has blended these three elements in unusual ways.

But there is a fourth stage in this narrative of constitutional development. This is achieved once it is recognized that, rather than being conceded from above, governmental authority is conferred from below. Authority is seen to derive neither from the sacred character of the office, nor from an acceptance of custom but comes directly from the people. Herein lies the peculiarity of British constitutional development. This last stage of modernization has not been realized through legal reconstruction but through political accommodation.

In this process, the law of the constitution retains its ancient form under which the highest authority in the land is the Crown-in-Parliament. But the legal powers of the crown are stripped from the monarch and made accountable to the people through evolving political practice. The crown's powers are now exercised by Ministers who must command the confidence of Parliament. This contest between political parties provides not only the means through which the government is rendered accountable to Parliament, it is also the vehicle for adapting governmental arrangements to the principle of democratic accountability. In the popular imagination, the highest authority in the land does not come from the abstraction of the Crown-in-Parliament: it is situated in a Victorian Gothic palace on the banks of the Thames at Westminster.

This ambiguous accommodation ensured that the British could make the transition to democracy without violent rupture. However, over the last century its limitations have been exposed and faith in the arrangement has suffered a progressive decline. Unsure of these customs, the British have been obliged to write down more and more in rules and regulations (Chapter 3). Uncertain of its role within big government, Parliament has ceased to act as 'mirror of the nation' and retains its pivotal status only because the British lack the political imagination for alternative ways of constituting authority (Chapter 4). With the growth of identity politics, the British—especially in the post-Brexit world—no longer express confidence in themselves as a nation that forms a state (Chapter 5). The tradition of protecting civil liberties through strict legality has collapsed, so liberty is bolstered by adopting an off-the-peg set of civil rights only to have that package placed in question (Chapter 6). Does a coherent set of rules, principles, and practices of governing any longer exist?

Constitutional interpretation

The authority of a constitution rests ultimately on the power of imagination, on the expression of a faith in nationhood and of how its system of government is envisioned. The system's rules are regularly revised by statutory reform and other formal changes. But vibrant constitutional practice also needs to harness the power of innovative re-interpretation. We have seen many illustrations of this in which the British pay tribute to ancient forms while continuously modernizing aspects of practice. But has the point been reached when governmental developments are imposing unbearable strains on narrative coherence, when discordant strands can no longer be drawn into a coherent story and when customary practices can no longer guide future conduct? Must the authority of experience now yield to the force of expectation?

The great constitutional scholars derived much of their confidence from belonging to the Victorian era when Britain ruled a mighty empire. Since then, there has never been a narrator to match the imaginative authority of the Whig historians or of Bagehot and Dicey. And over the last fifty years the mood has changed. Imaginative re-interpretation is being replaced by a growing demand for fundamental reconstruction. The constant refrain has become one of 'constitutional modernization'.

Modernization

If, as has been explained, most 20th-century writing about the constitution recognized that governing institutions continually change as British society and world conditions alter, what can 'modernization' signify? Though rarely made explicit, the term expresses growing dissatisfaction with these informal, evolving practices. It signifies the necessity of effecting a fundamental shift and adopting an altogether new British constitution built on a formal separation of legislative, executive, and judicial powers and the entrenched protection of basic rights. It signifies the need to abandon traditional practices and bring them into alignment with modern constitutional ideals.

This is a hazardous project. Such new settlements have only ever been instituted by states at moments of the fundamental breakdown of authority or of the birth of a new nation-state. They cannot easily be realized through incremental reform. In order to fit into the modern template, the role of these institutions will inevitably be distorted, leading to unintended negative consequences. Another problem is that government is required to take the initiative. But as Paine emphasized, a modern constitution, intended to be constitutive *of* government, cannot appropriately be made *by* government. The project certainly leads to more and more tacit understandings being replaced by formal rules, but whether the ostensible objective can be realized through this process of formalization must be doubted.

Parliamentary reform offers a good illustration of the first difficulty. Parliament is not easily slotted into the legislative role envisaged in a modern tripartite division of powers (Chapter 4). The first-past-the-post electoral system leads to an obvious skewing of its representational function. The adversarial mode in which its business is conducted ensures government dominance of the legislative timetable. The intense pressure on its timetable together with the peculiarities of its meeting times severely limit opportunities for deliberative scrutiny, and its cramped working conditions impede informed discussion. But whenever reform is contemplated, it is the legislative model that looms into view. Following the establishment of the Commons Modernization Committee in 1997, various reforms were instituted: streamlined procedures, more family-friendly sitting hours, improved timetabling that enabled uncompleted Bills to be carried over from one session to the next. During the Covid-19 pandemic there was experimentation with hybrid (online and in-person) procedures and proxy voting. These reforms may have made MPs better equipped to carry out some of their tasks, but they have done so at the cost of blunting certain instruments, such as the threat to continue debate late into the night or to filibuster a Bill, that have often been most effective in forcing governments to attend to parliamentary concerns.

As it has evolved, British constitutional practice works by holding governmental institutions in a relationship of mutual tension. If that tension is relaxed, vital constitutional aspects of the practice are lost. This has been the story of central–local government relations since 1980, when the centralization of powers in pursuit of efficiency undermined the sense of autonomy that justified local government as opposed to local administration. The problem also exists at the centre in the divide between a permanent, impartial civil service and transient, partisan ministers. Two agencies with different motivations, answerable to different constituencies and operating on different timescales, must work together to ensure that government decisions are clearly formulated and effectively implemented. Modernization in the name of efficiency has opened up civil service recruitment and led to the appointment of special advisers. Policy-making is pursued outside formal Whitehall processes and policy and operations are now formally divided, hiving off operational tasks to private or arm's-length bodies. But if the tight relationship between politicians and officials is destroyed, the costs can be substantial, not least a loss of trust in government when things go wrong.

Bringing in ministerial special advisers with the status of civil servants has blurred the distinction between official and politician and confused lines of accountability. Giving civil servants formal responsibility for decisions within their sphere of operations has eroded the ability of Parliament to test ministerial performance. Making policy in bilateral ministerial meetings rather than in Cabinet might be speedier but it erodes the collective responsibility of government. Driven by the desire to improve governmental effectiveness, modernization often leads to fragmentation and confusion of role.

Even when modernization is directed towards removing obvious anachronisms, there is a persistent tendency to avoid fundamental considerations. By all means modernize the monarchy by removing the rule of male-priority primogeniture, but removing religious discrimination in the law of succession? Perhaps that's a step too far. The monarchy bolsters government with the strength of religion, noted Bagehot, and 'when a monarch can bless it is best that she be not touched'. Mess with the protocols and the magic is lost. Subjecting the monarchy to a modern calculus of economy, efficiency, effectiveness, and equity is the surest way to its destruction.

It is not just the fate of one family that is at stake. In the slipstream of the royal train are any number of titles, privileges, and honours with political as well as social significance, not least with respect to the House of Lords. How can a modern democratic legislature persist with a second chamber containing hereditary peers? When the Parliament Act 1911 limited the powers of the Lords, its preamble stated the future intention to 'substitute for the House of Lords as it at present exists a Second Chamber constituted on a popular instead of hereditary basis'. No action to make good on that pledge has ever materialized. During the 20th century, it seemed that the Lords, poorly attended and sitting only a couple of days a week, would slowly die through debility. That was confounded in 1958 by the enactment of the Life Peerages Act, a reform that enabled the leaders of the main parties to stuff the House with patronage appointments, since when well over 1,000 life peers have been appointed. The reform had its progressive dimension: for the first time, women could participate in the House in significant numbers. But its main impact has been to rejuvenate the trade in political honours, to strengthen the power of party leaders, and to increase the power of an entirely unelected chamber.

Reforms were introduced in the House of Lords Act 1999. These removed the right of hereditary peers to sit but it then authorized them to elect 92 of their number to represent their interests in the House. Supposedly the first step towards comprehensive reform, all subsequent proposals have reached stalemate. A Bill for further reform was introduced by the Coalition government in 2012 but was withdrawn owing to a lack of support among Conservative backbenchers. And the Conservative 2019 manifesto pledged to establish a Constitution Commission whose remit would include review of the role of the House of Lords, but this pledge has not been acted on.

More than a century after an expressed intention to introduce a popularly elected second chamber, the House of Lords remains. Consisting of the 92 hereditary peers (now the only elected element!), 26 archbishops and bishops of the Church of England, and well over 600 appointed life peers, after the Chinese National People's Congress it is the second largest legislative assembly in the world. The continuing failure to address this embarrassing anomaly is symptomatic of a deeper malaise. It highlights the problem of leaving constitutional reform to government. While responsibility for implementation of reform continues to rest with those in power, the language of fundamental constitutional reform must remain, in Ferdinand Mount's fine phrase, 'the poetry of the politically impotent'.

Juridification

With the trend towards converting informal understandings into formal rules comes the challenge of legalization. We have seen various instances of this, including the attempt to persuade the court to enforce the Sewel convention once it had been placed on a statutory foundation and government efforts to ensure that the Ministerial Code not be given legislative force (Chapter 3). Yet there is no doubt that the declining authority of conventional practices has been a factor behind the growing significance of judicial review of governmental action. Perceiving the declining efficacy of parliamentary remedies, the judiciary, stated Lord Mustill in 1995, 'have had no option but to occupy the dead ground in a manner, and in areas of public life, which could not have been foreseen 30 years ago'. Modernization is contributing to the legalization of policy issues that fifty years ago were assumed to be beyond the judiciary's competence.

In the last chapter, we saw that the courts have engaged in judicial activism with the intention of re-ordering constitutional fundamentals. Their objective has been to rid themselves of the legacy of a Victorian mentality that maintained that judges sit merely 'as servants of the Queen and the legislature' (Willes, 1871) and to resurrect a juristic account of the British constitution. Invoking the spirit of the ancient constitution, the judiciary seeks to re-interpret 'the law of the constitution'. The constitution, it is asserted, is not some ineffable entity glimpsed fleetingly behind various laws and practices. It must now be conceived as a body of fundamental law ensuring that government operates in a manner that preserves liberty. Increasingly the judges maintain that the constitution is, in its essentials, the creation of the common law. Their task is to unpack the constitution as an ordered system of principles.

This requires a juridical shift of revolutionary proportions. The common law is no longer to be seen as proceeding from precedent to precedent, nor is it intrinsically subservient to statute. The very notion of the common law is rationalized. The concrete becomes abstract, precedent turns into principle, the protection of liberties is converted into the promotion of liberty, and jurisdictional control of governmental action is replaced by an abstract idea of legality as the fundamental legal principle of the constitution. The old 'constitution of liberty' becomes a new 'constitution of legality'.

This thesis, that of 'common-law constitutionalism', was explicitly presented by the late Sir John Laws. A leading Court of Appeal judge, he contended that sovereignty does not lie with 'those who wield governmental power'; rather, it rests 'in the conditions under which they are permitted to do so'. This is because it is the constitution, not the Parliament, that is sovereign. Laws follows through the logic of his claim by arguing that these conditions must be made explicit as 'a framework of fundamental principles'. This is a task for the judiciary, whose constitutional role must be to act as 'the guarantee that this framework will be vindicated'.

Following this lead, the courts now assert that there are such things as 'fundamental constitutional rights' which they must protect. These include rights of participation in the democratic process, equality of treatment, freedom of expression, the right to a fair trial, and the right of unimpeded access to the court. Judges maintain that they will vigilantly protect these fundamental rights, which cannot be overridden by Act of Parliament unless that intention is expressed in the clearest of terms. They also differentiate between Acts of Parliament by creating a new category of 'constitutional statutes', statutes that either regulate the relationship between citizen and state or enlarge or diminish the scope of fundamental rights. This category includes Magna Carta, the Bill of Rights 1689, the Treaty of Union 1707, the Representation of the People Acts, the Human Rights Act, and the devolution legislation. With respect to constitutional statutes, the judiciary asserts that amendment or repeal must be stated by Parliament explicitly; such changes are not to be imputed or presumed.

This judicial work-in-progress has received some support from Parliament, notably in the Constitutional Reform Act 2005 which institutionalizes a new understanding of the separation of powers. With judges routinely involved in reviewing governmental action, it was felt anachronistic that the highest court, the Appellate Committee of the House of Lords, remained part of the legislature while its judges, the Law Lords, could debate legislative proposals that might become the subject of litigation. The Law Lords had, by convention, maintained their distance from contentious legislative business, but the government concluded this was no longer sufficient. It proposed the establishment of a new Supreme Court for the UK as a formal expression of the principle of separation. This was enacted in Part III of the 2005 Act, and in Part II the opportunity was also taken to specify some of the conventions on judicial independence in statutory form.

In certain respects, the establishment of the Supreme Court was a typically British reform. The existing Law Lords simply upped sticks and, at great expense, moved out of the Palace of Westminster into newly refurbished accommodation across Parliament Square. But great efforts were made to heighten the symbolic significance of the move. The Justices took the initiative to modernize the working arrangements of the court, especially with respect to layout, costume, and accessibility. In place of the Baconian image of judges as lions under the throne, 'circumspect that they do not check or oppose any points of sovereignty', they devised as a new court emblem a wreath of entwined vegetation symbolizing the four nations of the UK with hardly a crown in sight.

The formation of the Supreme Court has bolstered the judiciary's confidence in articulating newly discovered fundamental principles of the constitution. In a remarkable innovation, section 1—apparently included through judicial lobbying—states that the Act 'does not adversely affect...the existing constitutional principle of the rule of law'. Since this 'constitutional principle' can only be determined by the judiciary, this gives considerable added impetus towards instituting legality as the fundamental principle of the British constitution.

The most significant evidence of this step was taken by the Supreme Court in 2019 in the case of *Miller v Prime Minister*. In the first *Miller* case—*Miller v Secretary of State for Exiting the EU* (2017)—the Supreme Court had held that the government was not authorized to trigger the notification of withdrawal from the EU by an exercise of its prerogative powers. Since rights were implicated, Parliamentary authorization was required. Coming in the immediate aftermath of a shock referendum result, it was a case that generated a great deal of heat. But despite exaggerated claims made for its significance, the ruling was relatively orthodox. The second *Miller* decision was not.

Miller II concerned the legality of a five-week prorogation of Parliament, covering the period immediately before final negotiations in the delivery of Brexit withdrawal. There is no statute or convention regulating the length of any prorogation which normally lasts 7 to 10 days. On occasions it has been longer, but the government maintained that only 7 to 10 sitting days would actually be lost since the period included the party conference season when Parliament adjourns for three weeks. Though the government did not command a parliamentary majority, no parliamentary action was taken to overturn this exercise of prerogative power. But its legality was challenged in both the English and Scottish courts and their two discrepant rulings were then appealed to the Supreme Court. In a single judgment, the eleven-member Court was unanimous. It held that a decision to prorogue Parliament would be unlawful if this had the effect of frustrating, without reasonable justification, Parliament's constitutional functions both as a legislature and as the institution responsible for holding the executive to account. The Court then declared that the PM had acted beyond his powers and that the prorogation was unlawful and of no effect.

The constitutional significance of this case arises from the Court's finding that the boundaries of a prerogative power are determined by 'the fundamental principles of our constitutional law'. Holding that the two most relevant constitutional principles are those of parliamentary sovereignty and parliamentary accountability, it invoked these principles to determine the limit of the power of prorogation and concluded that the PM had acted unlawfully. In doing so, the Court first re-interpreted such conventional practices as parliamentary accountability as 'normative principles' and then asserted its authority to act as the ultimate interpreter of their meaning. In this way, the Supreme Court took a vital step in proclaiming that the British constitution comprises a structure of legal principles which it is their singular responsibility to define and protect.

An impasse?

Rule formalization leads to juridification and this strengthens the judiciary's attempt to advance legality rather than sovereignty as the constitution's fundamental principle. In this project, the judiciary had been greatly assisted by the evolving processes of European integration. Holding neither the power of the sword nor the purse, the EU was obliged to rely on the use of formal rules and general principles to realize its aims. But that's not all. The UK's participation in the Council of Europe has required adherence to the principles of the European Convention on Human Rights. This means the acceptance of individuals' rights to petition the Court in Strasbourg and, through the Human Rights Act, the enforcement of those rights directly by domestic courts. This has further strengthened the judiciary's claim not just to be guardians of individual rights but also of constitutional principles.

What then does withdrawal from the EU portend? In other circumstances, Brexit might have become a constitutional moment, an occasion when the nation, recognizing a new chapter in the development of the British state, could have taken the opportunity to renovate constitutional fundamentals. But this was not to be. The referendum opened up new divisions within the nation and highlighted a gulf between the wishes of the majority and the views of their political representatives. Converting the decision into a policy became a treacherous process with major political risks.

What followed was a determined attempt by the government, in accordance with the political mantra of 'taking back control', to bolster the principle of sovereignty. In the EU (Withdrawal Agreement) Act of 2020, the government felt it necessary to include a provision that '[i]t is recognised that the Parliament of the United Kingdom is sovereign', that 'its sovereignty subsists' notwithstanding any continuing EU law, and that 'nothing in this Act derogates from the sovereignty of the Parliament of the United Kingdom' (s.38). This could be read simply as a technical clause within a complex transitional process. But it also sends a clear signal to the judiciary about constitutional ordering.

A similar trend could be discerned in their attempt in 2022–3 to replace the Human Rights Act with a Bill of Rights Act. Like the Dissolution and Calling of Parliament Act 2020, which repeals the Fixed-terms Parliament Act of 2011, revives the prerogative power to dissolve Parliament and makes it clear that the dissolution power is not justiciable, this measure was meant to recalibrate the balance of power between the legislature and the courts and bolster the sovereignty principle. Such initiatives are indicative of the emergence of a struggle between the government and the judiciary for the soul of the British constitution.

Constitutional modernization by governmental action undoubtedly has its flaws. But it should not be assumed that the judiciary fares much better. A glimpse into their understanding of the constitution can be gleaned from this succinct statement in *Miller II*:

> We live in a representative democracy. The House of Commons exists because the people have elected its members. The Government is not directly elected by the people (unlike the position in some other democracies). The Government exists because it has the confidence of the House of Commons. It has no democratic legitimacy other than that. This means that it is accountable to the House of Commons—and indeed to the House of Lords—for its actions, remembering always that the actual task of governing is for the executive and not for Parliament or the courts.

Such simplicities would have Bagehot spinning in his grave. Convened by the monarch for reasons of state, the House of Commons existed long before 'the people' in any meaningful sense elected its members. Ministers of the Crown exercise an authority that does not rest entirely on the confidence of the Commons. The representative democracy to which the Court refers works through a party system that determines parliamentary representation, meaning that the government is as directly elected by the people as in other democracies. While the government is, by convention, certainly accountable to the Commons, one cannot overlook the fact that one of the MPs' main functions—a function that determines the organization of Commons business—is to maintain the government and its supply. And the Court's afterthought about accountability to the Lords reveals just how attenuated this system of representative democracy is.

Nor can the peculiarities of 'common-law constitutionalism' be ignored. Scots law is different from the English common law. On one reading, the assertion of a common-law foundation to the constitution is a blatant, if less than explicit, appeal to English hegemony. Promoting such a distinctively English claim when British governmental arrangements have never been more differentiated scarcely makes political sense. But perhaps the claim to the supremacy of 'common law' is based on some abstract 'natural' rights claim rather than referring to English precedents? This would be to countenance a radical shift in constitutional foundations brought about by judges engaging in a scholastic exercise in political reasoning. The intention presumably is to blur these two distinct interpretations and advance 'common-law' claims founded not on precedents but on some idealized and rationalized reconstruction. If so, it requires us to place great faith in the political nous of the judiciary.

Some constitutional scholars have responded to this unsettled state of affairs by contending that British constitutional practice evolves through a continuing 'dialogue' or 'collaboration' between the main institutions of government. Yet recent developments reveal just how far from reality this contention is. Current relations between the government, Parliament, and the judiciary are indicative of a continuing struggle over competing conceptions of constitutional foundations. They signal an impasse that is destined to persist for some time to come.

References and further reading

Chapter 1: The existential question

Lord Hailsham, *The Dilemma of Democracy: Diagnosis and Prescription* (Glasgow: Collins, 1978).

Will Hutton, *The State We're In* (London: Cape, 1995).

Martin Loughlin, 'The British Constitution: Thoughts on the Cause of the Present Discontents' (2018) 16 *New Zealand J. of Public & International Law* 1–19.

David Marquand, *The Unprincipled Society: New Demands and Old Politics* (London: Fontana, 1988).

Tony Wright, *British Politics: A Very Short Introduction* (Oxford: Oxford University Press, 3rd edn., 2020).

Chapter 2: What constitution?

Edmund Burke, *Reflections on the Revolution in France* [1790], ed. C. C. O'Brien (London: Penguin, 1986).

Sir Alfred Denning, 'The Spirit of the British Constitution' (1951) 29 *Canadian Bar Review* 1180–95.

Nevil Johnson, *In Search of the Constitution: Reflections of State and Society in Britain* (Oxford: Pergamon Press, 1977).

C. H. McIlwain, *Constitutionalism: Ancient and Modern* (Ithaca, NY: Cornell University Press, rev. edn., 1947).

James Madison, Alexander Hamilton, and John Jay, *The Federalist Papers* 1787, ed. I. Kramnick (London: Penguin, 1987).

E. S. Morgan, *Inventing the People: The Rise of Popular Sovereignty in England and America* (New York: Norton, 1989).

Michael Oakeshott, *Rationalism in Politics and Other Essays* (London: Methuen, 1962).

Thomas Paine, *Rights of Man, Common Sense and Other Political Writings*, ed. M. Philp (Oxford: Oxford University Press, 1995).

T. B. Smith, 'The Union of 1707 as Fundamental Law' (1957) *Public Law* 99–121.

M. J. C. Vile, *Constitutionalism and the Separation of Powers* (Oxford: Clarendon Press, 1967).

Chapter 3: Writing the constitution

Walter Bagehot, *The English Constitution* (Oxford: Oxford University Press, 2001).

William Blackstone, *Commentaries on the Laws of England* (Oxford: Clarendon Press, 1776), vol. 1.

Andrew Blick, *UK Politics* (Oxford: Oxford University Press, 2021).

J. W. Burrow, *A Liberal Descent: Victorian Historians and the English Past* (Cambridge: Cambridge University Press, 1981).

John W. Cairns, 'Blackstone, an English Institutionalist: Legal Literature and the Rise of the Nation State' (1984) 4 *Oxford J. of Legal Studies* 318–60.

Edward Coke, *The Selected Writings and Speeches of Sir Edward Coke*, ed. S. Sheppard (Indianapolis: Liberty Fund, 2003), vol. 2.

S. Collini, D. Winch, and J. W. Burrow, *That Noble Science of Politics: A Study in Nineteenth-Century Intellectual History* (Cambridge: Cambridge University Press, 1983), ch. 5.

A. V. Dicey, *Introduction to the Study of the Law of the Constitution* (London: Macmillan, 8th edn., 1915).

E. A. Freeman, *The Growth of the English Constitution* (London: Macmillan, 1876).

James I, 'Speech to Star Chamber of 20 June 1616', in his *Political Writings*, ed. J. P. Somerville (Cambridge: Cambridge University Press, 1994), 204–28.

W. I. Jennings, *The Law and the Constitution* (London: University of London Press, 1933).

Jeffrey Jowell and Colm O'Cinneide (eds.), *The Changing Constitution* (Oxford: Oxford University Press, 9th edn., 2019).

David Judge, 'Would I Lie to You? Boris Johnson and Lying in the House of Commons' (2022) 93 *Political Quarterly* 443–63.

John P. Mackintosh, *The British Cabinet* (London: Stevens, 1962).

Montesquieu, *The Spirit of the Laws*, trans. and ed. A. Cohler,
    B. Miller, and H. Stone (Cambridge: Cambridge University Press,
    1989), Bk. 11, ch. 6.

Ferdinand Mount, *The British Constitution Now* (London:
    Heinemann, 1992), ch. 2.

J. G. A. Pocock, *The Ancient Constitution and the Feudal Law:
    A Study of English Historical Thought in the Seventeenth Century*
    (Cambridge: Cambridge University Press, rev. edn., 1987).

Ministerial Code, Civil Service Management Code, Cabinet Manual:
    online at www.gov.uk/government/publications/...Committee on
    Standards in Public Life: https://www.gov.uk/government/
    organisations/the-committee-on-standards-in-public-life

Independent Parliamentary Standards Authority: https://www.
    theipsa.org.uk/

R (Miller) v Secretary of State for Exiting the European Union
    [2017] UKSC 5.

R (FDA) v Prime Minister and Minister for the Civil Service [2021]
    EWHC 3279 (Admin).

2nd Report of the House of Commons Political and Constitutional
    Reform Committee Session 2014–15, *A New Magna Carta?*
    https://publications.parliament.uk/pa/cm201415/cmselect/
    cmpolcon/463/46302.htm

Chapter 4: Parliamentary government

Robert Blackburn and Andrew Kennon, *Griffith and Ryle on
    Parliament: Functions, Practice and Procedures* (London: Sweet &
    Maxwell, 2nd edn., 2003).

John Brewer, *The Sinews of Power: War, Money and the English State,
    1688–1783* (New York: Knopf, 1989).

G. R. Elton, *The Tudor Revolution in Government* (Cambridge:
    Cambridge University Press, 1953).

Keith Ewing, 'Covid-19: Government by Decree' (2020) 31 *King's
    Law J.* 1–24.

G. W. F. Hegel, 'The English Reform Bill', in his *Political Writings*,
    trans. T. M. Knox (Oxford: Clarendon Press, 1964), 295–330.

Peter Hennessy, *Cabinet* (Oxford: Blackwell, 1986).

Christopher Hill, *The Century of Revolution, 1603–1714* (London:
    Routledge, 2nd edn., 2001).

J. C. Holt, *Magna Carta* (Cambridge: Cambridge University Press,
    2nd edn., 1992).

Iain McLean, *What's Wrong with the British Constitution?* (Oxford: Oxford University Press, 2010), ch. 4.

Geoffrey Marshall, *Constitutional Conventions: The Rules and Forms of Political Accountability* (Oxford: Clarendon Press, 1984).

E. S. Morgan, *Inventing the People: The Rise of Popular Sovereignty in England and America* (New York: Norton, 1989).

Steve Pincus, *1688: The First Modern Revolution* (New Haven: Yale University Press, 2009).

Hannah White, *Held in Contempt: What's Wrong with the House of Commons?* (Manchester: Manchester University Press, 2022).

Martin Williams, *Parliament Ltd: A Journey to the Dark Heart of British Politics* (London: Hodder & Stoughton, 2016).

Chapter 5: Reconfiguring the state

T. R. S. Allan, 'Parliamentary Sovereignty: Law, Politics, and Revolution' (1997) 113 *Law Quarterly Review* 443–52.

Gerald Aylmer, 'The Peculiarities of the English State' (1990) 3 *Journal of Historical Sociology* 91–108.

Vernon Bogdanor, *Beyond Brexit: Towards a British Constitution* (London: I.B. Tauris, 2019).

Linda Colley, *Britons: Forging the Nation, 1707–1837* (New Haven: Yale University Press, 2005).

Oran Doyle, Aileen McHarg, and Jo Murkens (eds.), *Constitutions Under Pressure: The Brexit Challenge for Ireland and the United Kingdom* (Cambridge: Cambridge University Press, 2021).

Owen Dudley Edwards (ed.), *A Claim of Right for Scotland* (Edinburgh: Polygon, 1989).

Colin Kidd, *Union and Unionisms: Political Thought in Scotland, 1500–2000* (Cambridge: Cambridge University Press, 2008).

Martin Loughlin, 'The State, the Crown and the Law', in his *The Nature of the Crown: A Legal and Political Analysis*, ed. Maurice Sunkin and Sebastian Payne (Oxford: Oxford University Press, 1999), ch. 3.

Neil MacCormick, *Questioning Sovereignty* (Oxford: Oxford University Press, 1999), ch. 4.

Brendan O'Leary, *A Treatise on Northern Ireland*, 3 vols (Oxford: Oxford University Press, 2019)

Richard W. Rawlings, *Delineating Wales: Constitutional, Legal and Administrative Aspects of National Devolution* (Cardiff: University of Wales Press, 2003).

Sir John R. Seeley, *The Expansion of England* (London: Macmillan, 1925).

Uday Singh Mehta, *Liberalism and Empire: A Study in Nineteenth-Century British Liberal Thought* (Chicago: University of Chicago Press, 1999).

Robert Tombs, *This Sovereign Isle: Britain In and Out of Europe* (London: Allen Lane, 2021).

Sir William Wade, 'Sovereignty: Revolution or Evolution?' (1996) 112 *Law Quarterly Review* 568–75.

Stuart G. White, 'The Referendum in the UK's Constitution: From Parliamentary to Popular Sovereignty?' (2022) 75 Parliamentary Affairs 263–80.

Calvin's Case (1608) 7 Co. Rep. 1.

Costa v ENEL, Case 6/64 [1964] ECR 585.

R. v Secretary of State for Transport, ex parte Factortame (No. 2) [1991] 1 AC 603.

Van Gend en Loos v Nederlandse Administratie der Belastingen Case 26/62 [1963] ECR 1.

Chapter 6: Civil liberty

Tom Bingham, *The Rule of Law* (London: Penguin, 2011).

William Blackstone, *Commentaries on the Laws of England* (Oxford: Clarendon Press, 1776), vol. 1, Bk I, ch. 1.

David Clark and Gerard McCoy, *The Most Fundamental Legal Right: Habeas Corpus in the Commonwealth* (Oxford: Clarendon Press, 2000), ch. 2.

A. V. Dicey, *Introduction to the Study of the Law of the Constitution* (London: Macmillan, 8th edn., 1915), chs 4, 8.

Conor Gearty, *On Fantasy Island: Britain, Strasbourg and Human Rights* (Oxford: Oxford University Press, 2016).

Lord Hewart, *The New Despotism* (London: Benn, 1929).

H. J. Laski, 'Judicial Review of Social Policy in England' (1926) 39 *Harvard Law Review* 832–48.

Sir Stephen Sedley, 'The Sound of Silence: Constitutional Law without a Constitution' (1994) 110 *Law Quarterly Review* 270–91.

A. v Secretary of State for the Home Department [2004] UKHL 56.

Jackson v AG [2005] UKHL 56.

Malone v Metropolitan Police Commissioner [1979] Ch 344; *Malone v UK* (1984) 7 EHHR 14.

Chapter 7: Whither the constitution?

T. R. S. Allan, *Law, Liberty and Justice: The Legal Foundations of British Constitutionalism* (Oxford: Oxford University Press, 1994).

Eoin Daly, 'Constitutionalism and Crisis Narratives in Post-Brexit Politics' (2020) 68 *Political Studies* 895–915.

C. D. Foster, *British Government in Crisis* (Oxford: Hart, 2005).

House of Commons Modernization Committee, *Modernisation of the House of Commons: A Reform Programme*, HC 1168, Session 2001–2.

Sir John Laws, 'Law and Democracy' 1995 *Public Law* 72–93.

Public Administration Select Committee, *Taming the Prerogative: Strengthening Ministerial Accountability to Parliament*, HC 422, 4th Report, Session 2003–4.

Meg Russell, 'Brexit and Parliament: The Anatomy of a Perfect Storm' (2021) 74 *Parliamentary Affairs* 443–63.

Mark D. Walters, *A. V. Dicey and the Common Law Constitutional Tradition: A Legal Turn of Mind* (Cambridge: Cambridge University Press, 2020).

R (Miller) v Secretary of State for Exiting the European Union [2017] UKSC 5.

R (Miller) v Prime Minister/Cherry v Advocate General for Scotland [2019] UKSC 41.

Index

For the benefit of digital users, indexed terms that span two pages (e.g., 52–53) may, on occasion, appear on only one of those pages.